A Charge to Keep

A Charge to Keep

Gordon-Conwell Theological Seminary and
the Renewal of Evangelicalism

Garth M. Rosell

WIPF & STOCK · Eugene, Oregon

A CHARGE TO KEEP
Gordon-Conwell Theological Seminary and the Renewal of Evangelicalism

Wipf & Stock
An Imprint of Wipf and Stock Publishers
199 W. 8th Ave., Suite 3
Eugene, OR 97401

www.wipfandstock.com

PAPERBACK ISBN: 978-1-7252-5669-9
HARDCOVER ISBN: 978-1-7252-5670-5
EBOOK ISBN: 978-1-7252-5671-2

Manufactured in the U.S.A.   MARCH 3, 2020

Dedicated to our Founders

Billy Graham
Harold John Ockenga
J. Howard Pew

A Charge to Keep I Have

Words by Charles Wesley and Tune by Lowell Mason

A charge to keep I have, a God to glorify,
a never-dying soul to save, and fit it for the sky.

To serve the present age, my calling to fulfill,
O, may it all my pow'rs engage to do my Master's will!

Arm me with jealous care, as in Thy sight to live,
and O, Thy servant, Lord, prepare a strict account to give!

Help me to watch and pray, and on Thyself rely,
so shall I not my trust betray, nor love within me die.

Charles Wesley (1707–88), a leader of the Methodist movement, wrote approximately 6,500 hymns and Lowell Mason (1792–1872) composed some 1,600 hymn tunes including BOYLSTON, the traditional setting for this hymn. Mason also served from 1829–31 as the choirmaster and organist at Boston's historic Park Street Church, the congregation that Harold John Ockenga served as pastor during much of the twentieth century. Version taken from *The Asbury Hymnal* (Franklin, TN: Seedbed Publishing, 2018).

Contents

Preface

NOT LONG AFTER GORDON-CONWELL Theological Seminary cel-
ebrated its eighth birthday, President Harold John Ockenga wrote
a letter inviting me to join the seminary's faculty and to serve as its
Academic Dean.[1] Still in my thirties and having only recently cel-
ebrated an eighth anniversary of my own, teaching church history
at Bethel Theological Seminary, I was not at all sure I was ready
for a new assignment or even if I was willing to leave a community
where I would have been quite content to remain for a lifetime.
What convinced me to leave, however, was the absolutely breathtaking vision that President Ockenga described to me while we
talked together in a little restaurant in terminal B at Logan Airport
in Boston, Massachusetts.

It was a vision so comprehensive, so biblically centered, so
intellectually demanding and so spiritually compelling that it literally took my breath away! What President Ockenga described to
me on that memorable day, amid the noisy clamor of a busy airport, was nothing short of spiritually revolutionary—touching every square inch of God's creation, as Abraham Kuyper might have
described it, and demanding one's deepest commitment. Here was
no "business as usual" rhetoric. Rather, here was a prophetic call to
prepare a new generation of well-trained, spiritually mature, morally upright, Christ-centered, biblically literate, church-centered

---

1. Harold John Ockenga to Garth M. Rosell, March 22, 1978, and Rosell to
Ockenga, March 30, 1978, GMR Papers housed at the seminary.

and intellectually gifted men and women to spread the life-giving gospel to every man, woman, girl and boy on the face of the planet.

"I am the light of the world," Jesus Christ had proclaimed. "Whoever follows me will not walk in darkness, but will have the light of life."[2] Having purposely planted Gordon-Conwell Theological Seminary in the rich intellectual and spiritual soil of New England, its founders fully intended that the new seminary, to borrow the language of the region's first Puritan settlers, would become a shining "city on a hill"—a bright beacon proclaiming by word and deed that Christ is the one true light in a needy world.

> Called by its Master to be a *missionary light*, to share the Good News in word and deed to people of every tongue, tribe and nation around the globe;

> Called by its Master to be a *Bible light,* training students in Greek and Hebrew so that they would be able to study, rightly divide, proclaim and obey the Scriptures as the inerrant Word of God;

> Called by its Master to be a *revival light*, fostering spiritual renewal among individuals, churches and communities;

> Called by its Master to be an *evangelical light,* welcoming partnership with all who share a common authority (the Bible), a common experience (new birth), a common mission (worldwide evangelization) and a common vision (the spiritual renewal of church and society);

> Called by its Master to be a *Christ-centered light,* joining hands with all who share a burning love for Jesus and a passion to serve Him;

> Called by its Master to be a *united light*, calling a divided church to join head, hands and hearts in the service of its one true Head;

> Called by its Master to be a *purified light,* linking all who truly hunger and thirst after righteousness;

---

2. The Gospel of John 8:12 (ESV)

Called by its Master to be a *prophetic light*, calling a
troubled world to justice, righteousness and peace;

Called by its Master to be a *compassionate light*, caring
for all who are in need and treating each in the manner
we ourselves would want to be treated; and

Called by its Master to be a *thinking light*, eschewing all
forms of anti-intellectualism and dedicating its brightest
minds and deepest passions to the relentless search for
truth.

"We have a need of new life from Christ in our nation,"
President Ockenga was convinced, and "that need first of all is
intellectual." Unless "the Church can produce some thinkers who
will lead us in positive channels our spiral of degradation will
continue downward." Furthermore, he continued, "there is great
need in the field of statesmanship." Where are the political leaders
"in high places of our nation," he asked, with "a knowledge of and
regard for the principles of the Word of God?" The need is "even
more evident in the business world" where models of Christian
integrity have become such a rarity. Most of all, he concluded,
"there must be a new power in personal life. Unless this message
of salvation which we hold to be the cardinal center of our Christian faith really does save individuals from sin, from sinful habits,
from dishonesty, impurity and avarice, unless it keeps them in the
midst of temptation, what good is it? Christians today are altogether too much like the pagan and heathen world both in actions
and in life."[3]

President Ockenga's vision, drawn more from the first century than his own, is needed today perhaps more than ever. It is
that vision that drew me to the seminary. It is that vision that has
drawn dozens of godly, highly trained and internationally recognized scholars to its faculty. It is that vision that has attracted thousands of spiritually hungry students to the rigors and demands of
its classrooms. And it is that vision that continues to energize its

---

3. Harold John Ockenga, "Christ for America," *United Evangelical Action*
(May 4, 1943), 3–4, 6.

graduates to "attempt great things for God and to expect great things from God."

The story of Gordon-Conwell Theological Seminary deserves to be told—not, God forbid, to bring glory to itself, but to express its gratitude to the triune God who alone is deserving of its worship, gratitude and praise. As in every human institution, of course, there is much in the seminary's history that is unworthy of the God it was established to serve. Yet there is also much in the seminary's history that, however inadequate, is honoring to Christ and worthy of remembering.

As the seminary pauses to celebrate its first half-century of service, its founding vision, drawn from the pages of Holy Scripture, still holds the key (by God's grace) to the seminary's future: a future, as William Carey might have phrased it, that "is as bright as the promises of God."[4]

4. Quotations attributed to William Carey.

CHAPTER I

The History before the History

The farther backward you can look,
the farther forward you are likely to see.

—WINSTON CHURCHILL[1]

"GORDON-CONWELL THEOLOGICAL SEMINARY," as historian Nigel
Kerr liked to say, "stands as a monument to God's faithfulness."[2]
The merger in 1969 of Philadelphia's Conwell School of Theology
and Boston's Gordon Divinity School blended the strengths of
two much older but remarkably similar educational institutions:
Both founded in the 1880s; both started by Baptist ministers; both
rooted in the city (Philadelphia and Boston); both offering classes
at night so working folk could attend; both open from the very
beginning to women as well as men; both Bible-centered; and both
built upon the vision—as Russell Conwell phrased it—of making
"an education possible for all young men and women who have

1. Quotation used by President Robert E. Cooley on the occasion of his
installation as the second president of Gordon-Conwell Theological Seminary.
Contact, Inauguration Issue, Vol. 12, No. 1 (Winter 1981/1982)

2. William Nigel Kerr, "The First 25 Years" (published by Gordon-Conwell
Theological Seminary, January 1, 1995), 1.

good minds and the will to work" or as Adoniram Judson Gordon phrased it "of equipping men and women in practical religious work and furnishing them with a thoroughly Biblical training."[3]

The need for such education was obvious. The late nineteenth century was a time of enormous change within America and around the world. The rise of the city, the growth of industry and the emergence of new patterns of immigration were quite literally transforming the landscape of American life. With the explosive growth of Philadelphia and Boston, for example, urban pastors such as Conwell and Gordon were faced with a whole set of new problems and new opportunities. "Into our doors," observed A. J. Gordon in his 1887 address to the Evangelical Alliance in Washington, D.C., "the untaught and unregenerated populations of the Old World are pouring by the hundreds of thousands every year, while through our doors we can look out upon every nation of the globe as a field ripe for missionary harvest."

"The church according to its primitive ideal," Gordon continued, "is the one institution in which every man's wealth is under mortgage to every man's [need], every man's success to every man's service; so that no laborer in any part of the field should lack the means for prosecuting his work so long as any fellow-disciple in any other part of the field has ability to supply his lack." But "as surely as darkness follows sunset," Gordon warned, "will the alienation of the masses follow sanctimonious selfishness in the church. If a Christian's motto is, 'Look out for number one,' then let him look out for estrangement and coldness on the part of number two." Indeed, "it is not an orthodox creed which repels the masses, but an orthodox greed."[4]

3. Garth M. Rosell, "The Faithfulness of God" sections adapted for use in this chapter from the *Africanus Journal*, Vol. 8, No. 1 (April 2016), 7–13.

4. Adoniram Judson Gordon, "Individual Responsibility Growing out of our Perils and Opportunities," in *National Perils and Opportunities: The Discussions of the General Christian Conference of the Evangelical Alliance* held in Washington, D.C., December 7–9, 1887 (New York: Baker & Taylor, 1887), 379–81. I am indebted to my good friend, historian Grant Wacker, for drawing my attention to this important article.

In Philadelphia, to the south, Russell Conwell was expressing similar sentiments: Troubled by the growing problems of the poverty, hunger, unemployment, and despair he observed all around him, he could see "but one general remedy for all these ills"—namely, the provision of "a more useful education" for those who were in need. So it was, in 1884, that what Conwell came to call the "Temple College Idea" was born—and the tuition-free, Bible-centered, night school for working adults (eventually to be known as Temple University) was launched in the basement of the Temple Baptist church in Philadelphia. Within five years, it had a student population of over a thousand.[5]

Meanwhile in Boston, plans for a similar school were being laid. Thirty students (twenty men; ten women) gathered in the vestry of the Clarendon Street Church early in October of 1889, to help launch the Boston Missionary Training School. Established, as Gordon phrased it, to help "meet the demand for a large increase of our missionary force," the new school helped to train many generations of dedicated leaders for both church and society.[6]

The stories of these two remarkable institutions provide us with a fascinating "history before the history," so to speak, since each offered significant and essential contributions to the founding of Gordon-Conwell Theological Seminary.[7] Temple University,

5. James Hilty, *Temple University: 125 Years of Service to Philadelphia, the Nation, and the World* (Philadelphia: Temple University, 2009); "University Began as Theology School, 1884," *Temple University News* (Friday, November 2, 1962), 27; and Nigel Kerr, "The First 25 Years," 1–2.

6. Nathan R. Wood, *A School of Christ* (Boston: Halliday Lithograph Corporation and Robert Burlen and Son, 1953); Thomas A. and Jean M. Askew, *A Faithful Past & an Expectant Future: Celebrating a Century of Christian Higher Education* (Wenham, MA: Gordon College, 1988); Wendy Murray, ed., *Leading the Way: The Gordon College Legacy in Christian Higher Education* (Wenham, MA: Gordon College, 2014); and Scott M. Gibson, *A. J. Gordon: American Premillennialist* (Lanham, MD: University Press of America, 2001).

7. I have borrowed the phrase and chapter title, "History before the History," from George M. Marsden, *Reforming Fundamentalism: Fuller Seminary and the New Evangelicalism* (Grand Rapids: Eerdmans, 1988). See also Garth M. Rosell, ed., *The Vision Continues: Centennial Papers of Gordon-Conwell Theological Seminary* (South Hamilton, MA: Gordon-Conwell Theological Seminary, 1992).

as the school established by Russell Conwell in 1884 had come to be known, had grown to nearly fifty thousand students by the 1960s. The beloved old school of theology, however, was no longer an official part of the university structure since the acceptance of tax-funded government aid had made it necessary for the university to replace it in 1961 with a department of religion.[8]

Thanks largely to the generosity of the university and to the tenacious efforts of those who were convinced that the work of the school of theology needed to continue, the Conwell School of Theology, as it came to be called, was established and allowed to continue its work for a time on university property. "Be it resolved," voted the Trustees of Temple University in 1961, that the Conwell School of Theology "be permitted to use such resources and facilities of the University as are appropriate to its ends" including "libraries, advice, and consultation of the members of both bodies which would be destined to advance the strong academic interrelationships."[9] By the late 1960s, however, the growing need for additional space on campus and increasing pressure from some administrators within the university were making it painfully clear that the Conwell School of Theology, if it were to have a viable future, would need to move away from the campus and into its own facilities.

Along with the obvious difficulties of relocation and separation from the university, a long list of additional challenges confronted Stuart Barton Babbage in 1967 when he received and accepted "an unexpected invitation to accept the presidency of Conwell School of Theology." Among the most pressing problems were the seminary's loss of accreditation, its lack of funds, its need for new facilities, and its obvious need to recruit a first-rate faculty.

8. For an interesting account of this process see Stuart Barton Babbage, *Memoirs of a Loose Canon* (Brunswick East, Australia: Acorn Press, 2004), 137–62.

9. President Gladfelter, "Action of the Board of Trustees of Temple University," January 27, 1961. Copy in the Harold John Ockenga Papers housed at Gordon-Conwell Theological Seminary.

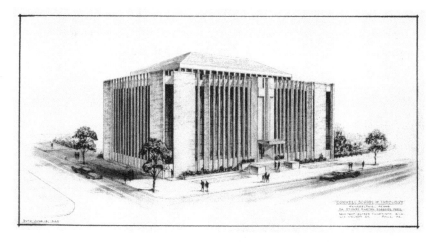

Plans for the Conwell School of Theology (never completed)

Among the new institution's most important assets, however, were the newest members of the seminary board. Daniel Poling, then editor of the *Christian Herald* and Vice-Chair of the Conwell School of Theology Board, had been successful in persuading both Billy Graham and J. Howard Pew to join the Conwell Board. "Billy Graham agreed to join the Board," as Babbage expressed it, "if Mr. Pew would guarantee substantial financial support and Mr. Pew agreed to join the Board if Billy Graham became Chairman."[10] While the addition of Graham and Pew brought new energy,

10. Babbage, *Memoirs*, 147–49. "Mr. Pew was nearing his nineties when I first met him," wrote Babbage. "Tall, upstanding, austere, inflexible, dogmatic and strongly right wing, he was a man of simple tastes and faith. A staunch Presbyterian, he owed his wealth to Sun Oil and generously supported a host of conservative causes, secular and religious. He was a major contributor to the Republican Party and, for thirteen years, continued to provide an annual subsidy of a quarter of a million dollars for Billy Graham's magazine, *Christianity Today*." Graham believed that about twelve million dollars would be needed for Conwell School of Theology "to cover the cost of new buildings and to provide a sufficient endowment for faculty." Pew, who was strongly opposed both to faculty tenure and institutional endowments, was happy to provide two million dollars for new buildings but nothing for endowments. The addition of Graham and Pew to the Conwell Board would prove to be crucial in making Gordon-Conwell Theological Seminary a reality.

enlarged visibility, and financial resources to the new institution, the task of securing new facilities and of building a new faculty fell on the willing shoulders of Stuart Barton Babbage.

Stuart Barton Babbage

Soon a beautiful old Victorian building, the Widener Mansion at Broad Street and Girard Avenue, was purchased not far from the Temple University campus for classrooms, library and offices.[11] Architectural plans were also prepared for a completely new seminary facility of sufficient size and design to accommodate up to four hundred students.[12] With office, library and classroom

---

11. For pictures and descriptions of the Weidner mansion see "Consulting Engineers Prepare Their Designs Where the Elite of Society Once Trod," *Consulting Engineer* (August 1966), 108–13.

12. The seminary was able to purchase a substantial number of books from New York's old Biblical Seminary library (predecessor of the New York Theological Seminary) to provide resources for the students.

space now available, Babbage turned his attention to faculty recruitment. Soon he was able to assemble a remarkably gifted group of teachers including Philip Edgecumbe Hughes in Biblical Languages and Literature, Stephen M. Reynolds in Old Testament, James R. Hiles in Old Testament Literature, Languages and Exegesis, Walter Mueller in New Testament Language and Literature, Graham Smith in Preaching, Robert Sproul in Theological Studies and Apologetics, Richard Lovelace in Historical Studies and Spiritual Renewal, Wesley Roberts in Church History and Black Studies, and Gary Collins in Pastoral Psychology.[13]

Studying theology in the heart of a great city proved to be both exhilarating and challenging for the fifty-five students who matriculated at the Conwell School of Theology in 1969. "North Philadelphia was like an armed camp in the late 1960s," wrote Bill Spencer, one of the students at the seminary. Assaults, robberies and shootings were regular occurrences in the neighborhood. Yet despite the challenges, he continued, most of my memories of the time I spent at the Conwell School of Theology "are endearing" and most of us as students realized that we "had something special here—this classic education engaged in the center of a contemporary metropolis."[14]

Meanwhile, nearly 350 miles to the north, over 280 students from thirty-three states and eleven countries were pursuing graduate studies in theology at Gordon Divinity School in Wenham, Massachusetts. Rumors of a possible merger between the two institutions were already in the air when on October 30, 1968, Harold John Ockenga, President Designate of Gordon

13. Drs. Hughes, Collins, Hiles, Lovelace, Sproul and Thorne made up the full-time faculty in 1968/1969 and Barraclough, Booth, Firster, Gast, Herr, Keefe, Mueller, Wyttenbach, Maser, Skinner, A. K. Smith and W. G. Smith taught part-time. See "Conwell School of Theology, Revised Budget for 1968–1969" in Harold John Ockenga Papers housed at Gordon-Conwell Theological Seminary. For reflections from one member of the faculty see Walter Mueller, "Reminiscences on the Early Days of Conwell School of Theology," in the *Africanus Journal*, Vol. 8, No. 1 (April 2016) 23–24.

14. William David Spencer, "The Seminary of the Future: Reflections on Gordon-Conwell Philadelphia (Former Student)," in the *Africanus Journal* (April 2006), 26–30.

College and Gordon Divinity School sent a letter to Stuart Barton Babbage, President of Conwell School of Theology, suggesting the possibility of a merger between the two seminaries.[15] Encouraged by Norman Klauder, Chairman of the Board of Conwell School of Theology, and Billy Graham, a member of Conwell's board, Babbage "warmly welcomed" the initiative.[16] "I seriously doubt if evangelical leaders have the financial or faculty resources for two major seminaries on the East Coast at this time," wrote Billy Graham in letter to Norman Klauder. "I believe a merger of these two institutions would immediately capture the imagination of evangelical Christians throughout the nation and we would find it much easier to raise funds." Furthermore, Graham continued, "it seems to me that the problems that we at Conwell have faced in getting a site for the seminary and a number of other problems that exist indicate that perhaps the Lord may be saying to us that this is the route we should follow. Therefore, I would like to enthusiastically endorse and vote for a proposal of merger."[17]

With this encouragement by key members of his board, President Babbage immediately began to prepare an organizational outline for consideration by the full board at a special meeting to be held on December 18, 1968. Noting five advantages for such a merger, he expressed his conviction that if accomplished, the merger would "make possible a rapid expansion and a development of the facilities of both schools, and inaugurate a period of rich and increasing usefulness."[18]

---

15. A copy of the letter can be found as part of the "Report on a SELF-STUDY Conducted by Gordon-Conwell Theological Seminary at the Request of THE ACCREDITING COMMISSION of THE AMERICAN ASSOCIATION OF THEOLOGICAL SCHOOLS, September 1970, 2–44.

16. For his account of the merger see Babbage, *Memoirs*, 152–56. Babbage suggests that it was "Glenn Barker's bold suggestion that the Conwell School of Theology merge with Gordon Divinity School in Massachusetts and move to a new location."

17. Graham to Klauder, December 9, 1968 in *GCTS Self-Study* (September 1970), Appendix 1, 11.

18. *GCTS Self-Study* (September 1970), Appendix 2, 2, 14–17.

Babbage was well aware, of course, that such a merger also carried significant risks, especially for the smaller institution. "As President," he reported to his faculty colleagues, "I made it clear that we were not interested in simply being absorbed in Gordon. I pointed out that we were interested in certain things which we desired to see safeguarded and preserved: that, at Conwell, we had sought to cultivate an attitude of openness to the world in which we live and a sensitive awareness of, and responsiveness to, the problems of our tortured society. In particular, we had sought to understand some of the intractable problems of the inner city, and had sought to open up lines of communication with the black community. The representatives of Gordon stated that they also were eager to share these concerns."[19]

So it was that in early February of 1969, the Board of Trustees of the Conwell School of Theology (at its meeting on February 3rd) and the Board of Trustees of Gordon College and Divinity School (at its meeting on February 10) both voted to move forward with the merger.[20] Under a letter of intent, they established a Joint Board made up of nine representatives from Conwell and nine representatives from Gordon.[21] At its first meeting, held on June 18, 1969, the Joint Board approved an "Instrument of Agreement" for consideration by the full boards of both the Conwell School of Theology and the Gordon Divinity School. On June 25, 1969 the "Instrument of Agreement" was approved by vote of the Board of Trustees of the Conwell School of Theology and on June 27, 1969 was similarly approved by the Board of Trustees of Gordon College and Gordon Divinity School. Having been formally approved by both boards, the "Instrument of Agreement" was

---

19. Babbage, *Memoirs*, 154.

20. See *GCTS Self-Study* (September 1970), 2–24 for the relevant documents and description of the sequence of events.

21. The representatives from Gordon were Arthur S. DeMoss, Billy Graham, H. Stewart Gray, Wesley G. Huber, Arthur C. Kenison, Robert Lamont, Harold Lindsell, Kenneth H. Olsen and Charles N. Pickell. The representatives from Conwell were David W. Baker, G. Kurt Davidyan, Allan C. Emery, Jr., William Eerdman, Leighton Ford, Norman Klauder, Walter Martin, Arthur N. Morris, and J. Howard Pew.

signed on June 27th by Harold J. Ockenga (representing Gordon College and Gordon Divinity School) and Stuart Barton Babbage (representing the Conwell School of Theology).[22] On September 1, 1969, "the two institutions began to function operationally as Gordon-Conwell Theological Seminary.[23]

Despite the enormous challenges involved in merging two proud old institutions from two different cities—to say nothing of the painstaking work of untangling the complex financial and personal issues involved in the process—the new seminary began to flourish and enjoy the blessing of God. A new campus was purchased, Gordon College and Gordon Divinity School were divided into two separate corporations, a new educational institution named Gordon-Conwell Theological Seminary was created, a new Board of Trustees was elected, a new faculty was assembled, new buildings were constructed, a new president was installed and prospective students began to take notice. Between the Fall Semester of 1969 (the start of the seminary's first year of operation) and the Fall Semester of 1979 (at the close of Harold John Ockenga's decade-long presidency) the number of credit students on the Hamilton campus had increased from 279 to 663.[24]

On October 22, 1969, Harold John Ockenga was officially installed as Gordon-Conwell Theological Seminary's first president in a gala celebration held in the heart of Boston.[25] The merger "is a milestone in evangelical theological education," remarked the

22. An original copy of the signed document, seven pages in length, along with the other documents referenced above can be found in the Harold John Ockenga Papers housed at Gordon-Conwell Theological Seminary.

23. *GCTS Self-Study* (September 1970), 8. The author also wishes to express a special word of appreciation to Dr. Richard Gross, the former Academic Dean and President of Gordon College, for his help in sorting through many aspects of the merger in an oral history interview conducted with the author and Dr. David Horn on April 17, 2018.

24. For a statistical breakdown see Garth M. Rosell, "Report to the President for the October Meeting of the Board of Trustees," October 4–5, 1984 in the Harold John Ockenga Papers housed at Gordon-Conwell Theological Seminary.

25. Ockenga had already been installed as President of Gordon College and Gordon Divinity School on April 1, 1969.

new president, combining resources from "two fine theological seminaries" into "what promises to result in one of the outstanding divinity schools in the world."[26] In addition to the installation of a new president, the board appointed Stuart Barton Babbage to serve as the new seminary's second in command. Under his guidance, the newly merged faculty began its work—blending five members of the old Conwell School of Theology faculty with the sixteen members of the old Gordon Divinity School faculty who were already here.[27] The board also authorized the purchase of the Hamilton campus from the Carmelites, established a Long-Range Planning Committee for "exploring ways and means of fulfilling some of the purposes of the merger" and approved the establishment of an urban center in Philadelphia.[28]

26. Harold John Ockenga as reported in "Gordon Merges With Pa. Theology School," in a local newspaper, the *Times* (April 14, 1969), 3. Clipping in the Harold John Ockenga Papers housed at Gordon-Conwell Theological Seminary.

27. The five from Philadelphia that chose to come north were Babbage, James R. Hiles, Philip E. Hughes, Richard Lovelace, and Stephen Reynolds. Those from Gordon Divinity School were Glenn W. Barker, Lit-Sen Chang, George Ensworth, Robert Fillinger, Burton Goddard, Lloyd Kalland (who assisted the transition for a time as acting dean), Deane Kemper, William Nigel Kerr, Meredith G. Kline, William L. Lane, Addison H. Leitch, J. Ramsey Michaels, Roger R. Nicole, Charles G. Schauffele, David M. Scholer, and Gwyn Walters.

28. Gordon-Conwell Theological Seminary operated an urban campus in Philadelphia during the 1969–70 academic year. During the 1970–71 academic year, an Institute for Black Ministries was established by the Council of Black Clergy "as a place where the full complement of seminary subjects would be taught—all from a black point of view." See Joseph Adcock, "Institute Furnishes Home for the New 'Black Theology,'" *Washington Post* (February 6, 1971), 10. The Philadelphia property was sold to the Institute for $1.

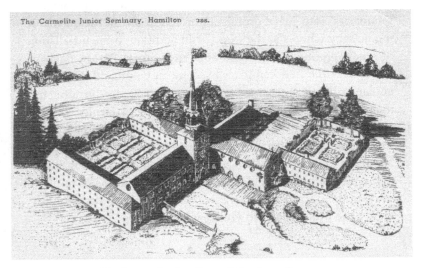

The Future Gordon-Conwell Seminary Campus

The very first official catalog—published for 1970/1971 academic year—described the new seminary with the following words:

> This is the first catalog describing the newly created Gordon-Conwell Theological Seminary. Gordon-Conwell has a vital concern for the ministry of the local church as well as all other types of effective witness.
>
> Men and women are prepared for service in urban, suburban and rural ministries. Along with a stress on academic excellence, Gordon-Conwell has a deep interest in the practical application of biblical truth and in the spiritual development of its students.

"At the present time there are two campuses," the catalog continued:

> The central campus is in Wenham, Massachusetts, and the urban center is in Philadelphia. During the course of the 1970–1971 academic year, Gordon-Conwell plans to move to its new campus, the 120-acre Carmelite Junior Seminary in Hamilton, just one and one-half miles from the main entrance of the Wenham campus. The purchase

is being made from the Fathers of the Carmelite Order. This facility contains everything necessary for a school of several hundred students. The one basic need is a library. Plans are in process for the erection of this building.[29]

Harold John Ockenga and Burton Goddard in front of the new Goddard Library

So it was that classes got underway in the fall of 1970 with a faculty of twenty-five (including administrative faculty), a student body of 320, tuition of $170/course, an eighteen-member Governing Board, a thirty-six-member Board of Trustees and courses leading to three degrees (the Master of Divinity, the Master of Religious Education and the Master of Theological Studies).

Without the vision, institutional savvy, and good old-fashioned hard work of two remarkable individuals, however, it is unlikely that the merger would ever have taken place or that Gordon-Conwell Theological Seminary would ever have come into existence. While others assisted in making the merger a reality (most especially,

29. Gordon-Conwell Theological Seminary, *Catalog for 1970–1971*, 10.

The Founders Harold John Ockenga and Billy Graham

perhaps, J. Howard Pew, whose amazing generosity helped to keep the school financially afloat during those early years, and Stuart Barton Babbage, whose administrative savvy moved the negotiations forward), two men in particular—Harold John Ockenga and Billy Graham—surely deserve "pride of place" in the founding of the new institution. Without them, humanly speaking, Gordon-Conwell Theological Seminary simply would not exist.[30] Indeed, it was the shared educational and missional vision of Ockenga and

---

30. George F. Bennett, *Memoirs of a Long Life* (Hingham, MA: privately printed, 2008), 111–12; Garth M. Rosell, *The Surprising Work of God: Harold John Ockenga, Billy Graham and the Rebirth of Evangelicalism* (Grand Rapids: Baker Academic, 2008) and "The Ockenga Vision" *Contact* (Vol. 30, No. 1), 3–6, 10–11, 20–21.

Graham that set the tone, excited the imagination and opened the way for the establishment, as Ockenga phrased it, of "one of the outstanding divinity schools in the world."

CHAPTER II

The Founders

This generation of Americans has a rendezvous with destiny.

—FRANKLIN DELANO ROOSEVELT[1]

IN HIS BESTSELLING BOOK, *The Greatest Generation*, Tom Brokaw recounts some of the stories of the men and women who "came of age during the Great Depression and the Second World War." United by a "common purpose" and "common values" such as "duty, honor, economy, courage, service, love of family and country, and, above all, responsibility for oneself," he argued, they succeeded both in building "modern America" and in giving to the world such advancements in science, literature, art, industry, and economic strength as are "unparalleled in the long curve of history." They are quite simply, Brokaw was convinced, "the greatest generation any society has ever produced."[2]

1. Franklin Delano Roosevelt, Acceptance Speech for a second term in office at the Democratic Convention in Philadelphia, Pennsylvania, June 27, 1936.

2. Tom Brokaw, *The Greatest Generation* (New York: Random House, 1998), from the dust jacket. Portions of this chapter are adapted from Garth M. Rosell, "The Ockenga Vision," in *Contact: The Ministry Magazine of Gordon-Conwell Theological Seminary*, Vol. 30, No. 1 (Summer 2000), 3–6, 10–11,

Such a bold appellation, of course, is a matter for debate. The achievements of that generation, however, are beyond question. Those born between 1901 and 1924, the so-called "G. I. generation," became by mid-century America's most powerful and influential economic, political, and religious leaders. Whether fighting wars, building roads, starting new businesses, getting elected to political office, landing astronauts on the moon, or winning Nobel prizes, their energy and optimism dominated the cultural landscape for the rest of the twentieth century.[3]

This was also the generation, of course, that provided fresh leadership for America's resurgent evangelical movement—founding dozens of new evangelical institutions, building hundreds of churches and reseeding old denominations, feeding the hungry and housing the orphans, writing books and publishing magazines, producing films and filling the airwaves, sending out missionaries and translating the Bible, building clinics and filling them with nurses and doctors, repairing damaged homes and providing clean water, establishing schools and founding theological seminaries like Fuller and Gordon-Conwell.[4] While many new leaders rose to prominence within the rapidly burgeoning movement, however, two remarkable individuals—Billy Graham and Harold John Ockenga—seemed to stand head and shoulders above the rest during the last half of the twentieth century. By 1945, Ockenga was widely known as "Mr. Evangelical" and a decade later, as historian George Marsden has suggested, the broadest and perhaps most universally

20–21 and Garth M. Rosell, *The Surprising Work of God* (Grand Rapids: Baker Academic, 2008), 11–38, 73–106.

3. See David M. Kennedy, *Freedom from Fear: The American People in Depression and War, 1929–1945* (New York: Oxford University Press, 1999); and William Strauss and Neil Howe, *Generations* (New York: William Morrow, 1991), 261–78.

4. Wesley K. Willmer and J. David Schmidt, *The Prospering Parachurch* (Hoboken, NJ: Jossey-Bass, 1998). The new generation, born between 1901 and 1924, included Ockenga (1905–85), Graham (1918–2018), Carnell (1919–67), Henry (1913–2003), and a variety of others. The older leadership, including Machen (1881–1937), Riley (1861–1947), Sunday (1862–1935), Macartney (1879–1957), Fuller (1887–1968), Torrey (1856–1928), Booth (1829–1912), and a host of others, had all been born prior to 1900.

accepted definition of an evangelical was simply "anyone who likes Billy Graham."[5]

United by a shared theological focus (the cross), a shared authority (the Bible), a shared experience (new birth), a shared mission (worldwide evangelization) and a shared vision (the spiritual renewal of the church and society), Ockenga and Graham developed a deep friendship and they joined hands to create dozens of new institutions and to promote scores of evangelical projects. "Outside my family, nobody influenced me more than he did," Graham told those who had gathered for Ockenga's funeral on a chilly February morning in 1985. "I never made a major decision without first calling and asking his advice and counsel." He was a "giant among giants in his generation," and "I thank God for his friendship and his life."[6]

The beginnings of Gordon-Conwell Theological Seminary owe more than a little to the unique blending of geographical regions, theological perspectives, collegial networks, personal styles, and ministerial experiences of these two remarkable individuals. Born and raised in Chicago, educated in the Midwest and Northeast, and based for most of his professional life in New England, Ockenga became the embodiment of what the old Puritans would have called the "learned pastor."[7] Born in Charlotte, educated in

5. George M. Marsden, *Understanding Fundamentalism and Evangelicalism* (Grand Rapids: Eerdmans, 1991), 6.

6. Billy Graham, "Harold John Ockenga: A Man Who Walked with God," *Christianity Today* (March 15, 1985), 35. See also Rosell, *The Surprising Work of God*, 13.

7. Born July 6, 1905, Harold John Ockenga was the only son of Herman and Angie Ockenga. Herman Ockenga worked for the Chicago Transit Authority and was a sometime grocer. Harold's mother, a devout Methodist, had him baptized in the nearby Austin Presbyterian Church. She and the children often attended the Olivet Methodist Church, on Chicago's west side, where, at the age of eleven, Harold John became a member. Converted in 1916 at an old-fashioned Methodist campground in Des Plaines, Illinois, he went on to pursue academic degrees and/or studies at Taylor University (1923–27), Princeton Theological Seminary (1927–29), Westminster Theological Seminary (1929–30), and the University of Pittsburgh (completing the M.A. degree in 1934 and the PhD degree in 1939).

the South and Midwest, and based for most of his professional life in the mountains of North Carolina, Graham came to embody not only the gracious piety of Southern evangelicalism but also the revival fervor and fresh enthusiasm of the great youth movements of the 1930s and 1940s.[8]

The combination of these two much older religious cultures, forged in the powerful spiritual awakening that was sweeping across America and around the world during the mid-twentieth century, helped give shape and substance to a resurgent evangelical movement. Linking the steepled church with the revival tent, the aroma of candles with the smell of sawdust, the passion for personal holiness with the love of truth, the quest for purity with the yearning for unity, the comfort of structure with the fresh winds of the Spirit, the majestic organ with the singing saxophone, the three-piece suit with the blue denim jacket, and the first-world with the Global South, the contemporary evangelical movement, as Alister McGrath suggested in 1995, "seems set to continue its upswing into the next millennium."[9]

With their distinctive backgrounds, both Harold John Ockenga and Billy Graham found ways of blending their unique strengths and priorities into a powerful vision for the new seminary. Ockenga's strong academic background, pastoral experience, and proven record of institutional leadership, brought academic

8. Born November 7, 1918, William Franklin Graham Jr., known in the early years as "Billy Frank" and later as "Billy," was the oldest of William Franklin and Morrow Coffey Graham's four children. His parents belonged to the Associate Reformed Presbyterian Church in Charlotte, where he was baptized, and they ran a successful four hundred-acre dairy farm. Converted in September of 1934 at a Mordechai Fowler Ham evangelistic crusade, Graham attended Bob Jones College, the Florida Bible Institute, and Wheaton College. Although he pastored a Baptist church in Western Springs, Graham became increasingly involved with Youth for Christ and eventually agreed to serve on its staff. Grant Wacker, *America's Pastor: Billy Graham and the Shaping of a Nation* (Cambridge: Belknap Press: An Imprint of Harvard University Press, 2014); *One Soul at a Time* (Grand Rapids, MI: Eerdmans, 2019), William C. Martin, *A Prophet with Honor: The Billy Graham Story* (Grand Rapids: Zondervan, 2018), updated edition.

9. Alister McGrath, *Evangelicalism and the Future of Christianity* (Downers Grove, IL: InterVarsity, 1995), 10–11.

credibility, theological *gravitas,* and recognized stature to the fledgling school. Graham's understanding of youth culture, his irenic spirit and his passion for evangelism brought fund-raising savvy, personal winsomeness, and thousands of potential students to the new institution.

The creative uniting of their remarkable gifts, made possible by a rock-solid friendship and deepening trust, opened the way for something quite unique: namely, the founding of a seminary that united head, heart, and hands—valuing the mind, serving the church, respecting the academy, focusing on serious study of the Bible (in the original languages), committed to the classical disciplines, concerned to promote the development of Christian character, convinced that biblical truth applies to every arena of life, passionate about the spread of the Christian gospel throughout the world, sensitive to the realities of the surrounding culture, devoted to peace and justice, centered on Christ and his atoning work on the cross, and committed to historic Christianity as reflected in the Scriptures, the confessions, and the classic creeds of the church. They were convinced that God deserves nothing less, as Gregory the Great had argued many centuries before, than our best thinking, our deepest devotion and our obedient service.

Billy Graham

Graham's early ministry, focused largely on American youth, had begun during the 1940s in the midst of a season of religious revivals that J. Edwin Orr has called "The Mid-Twentieth Century Awakening."[10] Such revivals were nothing new, of course. From the earliest years of European settlement in the New World, revivals of religion had become a familiar part of America's spiritual landscape.

---

10. J. Edwin Orr, *The Second Evangelical Awakening in America* (London: Marshall, Morgan & Scott, 1952), 188–211; quotation taken from 202.

Billy Graham Speaking in the Seminary Chapel

During certain eras, however, such occurrences had become so numerous and widespread as to be called "great awakenings."[11] It seems likely, across its history, that America has experienced at least four such unusual periods of awakening: beginning with the work of George Whitefield, Jonathan Edwards, Gilbert Tennent, and others in what is usually called "The Great Awakening" of the eighteenth century;[12] and continuing with the "Second Great Awakening" of the late-eighteenth and early-nineteenth centuries through the work of evangelists like Charles G. Finney and Asahel Nettleton;[13] and emerging yet again in the late-nineteenth and early twentieth centuries with the "Prayer Revival" of 1857,[14]

11. David Horn & Gordon L. Isaac, eds., *Great Awakenings: Historical Perspectives for Today* (Peabody, MA: Hendrickson, 2016).

12. Thomas S. Kidd, *The Great Awakening: The Roots of Evangelical Christianity in Colonial America* (New Haven, CT: Yale University Press, 2009).

13. Garth M. Rosell and Richard A. G. Dupuis, *The Memoirs of Charles G. Finney: The Complete Restored Text* (Grand Rapids: Zondervan, 1989) and Bennet Tyler, *Asahel Nettleton: Life and Labours* (Carlisle, PA: The Banner of Truth Trust, 1996).

14. Kathryn Teresa Long, *The Revival of 1857–58* (New York: Oxford University Press, 1998). Dr. Long is a graduate of the seminary.

the ministry of D. L. Moody,[15] the Welsh revival,[16] the Korean revival,[17] and (perhaps most notably) the great Pentecostal revivals that spilled outward from Azusa Street in Los Angeles in 1906 to literally change the shape and direction of world Christianity.[18]

A "Fourth Great Awakening," as some have called it, was beginning to emerge during the 1940s at the very time that Billy Graham was launching his own ministry.[19] And like many movements across Christian history—most notably, perhaps, being the story of the modern missionary movement—these early stirrings of revival began with the nation's youth.[20] Between World War I (1914–18) and World War II (1939–45), in fact, scores of new organizations, geared primarily to evangelize and disciple young men and women, had been established throughout North America: including Inter-Varsity Christian Fellowship of Canada (1928), the Christian Youth Campaigns for America (1929), the Young People's Church of the Air (1930), the Navigators (1933), the Christian Service Brigade (1937), the Voice of Christian Youth (1937), Young Life Campaign (1937), Pioneer Girls (1939), Inter-Varsity Christian Fellowship of the United States (1941), and Word

15. Lyle W. Dorsett, *A Passion for Souls: The Life of D. L. Moody* (Chicago: Moody Press, 1997) and Garth M. Rosell, ed., *Commending the Faith: The Preaching of D. L. Moody* (Peabody, MA: Hendrickson, 1999.

16. S. B. Shaw, *The Great Revival in Wales*, Jawbone Digital, December 2, 2012.

17. Daniel M. Weaver, *Pyongyang Revival* (Dickinson, ND: Revival Publishing, 2017).

18. Grant Wacker, *Heaven Below: Early Pentecostals and American Culture* (Cambridge: Harvard University Press, 2003) and Cecil Robeck Jr., *The Azusa Street Mission and Revival* (Nashville: Thomas Nelson, 2017).

19. These times of spiritual refreshment were certainly not limited to North America. Reports of religious revivals during these years can be found from Asia, Africa, India, Europe and Latin America. See for example, J. Edwin Orr, "World Survey of Spiritual awakening," appendix E, in *The Second Evangelical Awakening*, 202–11. For a more recent account see Mark Shaw, *Global Awakening: How 20th-Century Revivals Triggered a Christian Revolution* (Downers Grove, IL: InterVarsity Press, 2010).

20. Joel A. Carpenter, *Revive us Again* (New York: Oxford University Press, 1997), 161–76.

of Life (1941), to name but a few. The collective impact of these ministries was enormous.

During the 1940s, however, no Christian outreach to young men and women was more successful than was Youth for Christ, International (YFC). Its explosive growth was breathtaking, its global vision was ahead of its time, and its enormous influence surprised even its most ardent supporters. The ministry of YFC, in fact, helped to prepare the way for the great city-wide crusades that began to sweep across America and around the world during the early 1950s by providing much of its infrastructure, most of its leadership and nearly all of its most prominent evangelists. With rare exception, the cities with the strongest YFC presence in the 1940s became the venues most deeply touched by the revivals of the 1950s.[21]

While Chicagoland Youth for Christ held some of the most successful youth rallies, dozens of cities across America began to experience similar results as the Saturday night YFC events began to draw tens of thousands of young people into the largest auditoriums in city after city. Since all of these rallies included preaching, the most popular speakers—like Jimmie Johnson, Bob Cook, T. W. and Grady Wilson, Jack Shuler, Merv Rosell, Torrey Johnson, Percy Crawford, Jack Wyrtzen, and Billy Graham, to name a few—were increasingly in demand. This amazing "Band of Brothers" not only developed the ability to preach to large crowds but many of them became lifelong friends. Those friendships were further strengthened in 1948 when Youth for Christ, International held its first Congress for World Evangelization at a Bible School in Beatenberg, Switzerland. That historic gathering brought together a veritable "Who's Who" of evangelical leaders from around the world and it opened the way for new partnerships in the task of spiritual renewal within both church and culture.[22]

21. James C. Hefley, *God Goes to High School* (Waco, TX: Word, 1970), 13–27; and Bruce Shelley, "The Rise of Evangelical Youth Movements," *Fides et Historia* (January 1986), 47–63.

22. For a further description of the Congress on World Evangelization at Beatenberg, Switzerland see Garth M. Rosell, *The Surprising Work of God*, 107–59. Those attending the conference included Bob Pearce, Torrey Johnson,

Harold John Ockenga

Among the delegates at the Beatenberg gathering were Harold John Ockenga and Billy Graham. Although they had likely met previously, they certainly were not well acquainted. In fact, Ockenga had earlier decided against inviting Graham to preach in Boston since he was not sure that Graham's colorful ties and youthful style would go over well within the eastern culture. Beatenberg, however, began to change Ockenga's thinking and by 1949 he was ready to invite Graham for a New Year's Eve service at Boston's Mechanics Hall followed by a series of evangelistic services at Park Street Church during early January of 1950. Even then, despite the enormous success of Graham's late 1949 "watershed" crusade in Los Angeles, Ockenga and his colleagues in Boston were still not prepared for what they were about to experience in Boston.[23]

The New Year's Eve service at Mechanics Hall changed everything. The six thousand who jammed the hall, along with the hundreds of people who were turned away, suddenly made the event front-page news. "Evangelist Graham Draws 6000," proclaimed the *Boston Herald*, and "more than could be counted hit the sawdust trail," reported the *Boston Daily Globe*.[24] The *Boston Post*, in its Sunday edition, carried a full report of the four-hour meeting along with a detailed description of the service, a listing

---

Billy Graham, Merv Rosell, Charles E. Fuller, Harold John Ockenga, Amy Lee Stockton, Bob Cook, "Daws" Trotman, Oswald J. Smith and a host of others. For background on Harold John Ockenga see Harold Lindsell, *Park Street Prophet: A Life of Harold Ockenga* (Wheaton: Van Kampen Press, 1951) and John Adams, "The Making of a Neo-Evangelical Statesman," doctoral dissertation, Baylor University, 1994. For Ockenga's publications see Garth M. Rosell, Series Editor, *Harold John Ockenga: Voice of American Evangelicalism*, reprints of six of Ockenga's major writings, published by Wipf & Stock, Eugene, Oregon.

23. Harold John Ockenga, "Boston Stirred by Revival," *United Evangelical Action*, January 15, 1950, 2, 4, 15; *Revival in our Time: The Story of the Billy Graham Evangelistic Campaigns*, (Wheaton: Van Kampen Press, 1950), 28–33.

24. W. E. Playfair, "Evangelist Graham Draws 6000 from 'Eve' Celebration," *Boston Herald*, January 1, 1950, 1, 5; and "Graham Scores Typical Revelry of New Year's Eve," *Boston Daily Globe*, January 1, 1950, 1, 9.

of its major participants and a dramatic picture of the crowd that had filled Mechanics Hall to overflowing.[25]

One of the speakers that evening was Harold John Ockenga. In his address, "The Mid-Century Turning Point," he told his listeners that they were standing "at the division of the century." Looking back, he reminded his audience of "the stupendous changes" of the past fifty years. Then, looking forward, he pointed to "overwhelming evidence" that "God is visiting America." In Los Angeles, he continued, "the young evangelist speaking in this hall tonight, Billy Graham, began what was announced and planned to be a three-week campaign in a tent holding 5,000 people. From the beginning the tent was packed. Later 1,500 more chairs were added and night after night for eight weeks the tent was filled and people stood by the thousands." Turning his attention back to Boston, Ockenga then laid before the assembled crowd the possibilities that stretched out before them. "The hour for revival has struck, New England is ripe here," Ockenga declared. "Yesterday has gone. Tomorrow is uncertain. We have only today. Now is the time. Let us redeem it. Let us use it. Let us make it the vehicle of a glorious future in which Christian truth and experience will be spread abroad to become incorporated in the lives of us all."[26]

25. *Boston Post*, January 1, 1950, 15.

26. Harold John Ockenga, "The Mid-Century Turning Point," sermon 1448, preached at Mechanics Hall, December 31, 1949, Harold John Ockenga Papers housed at Gordon-Conwell Theological Seminary. For a more detailed presentation of Graham's 1950 meetings in Boston and throughout New England see Rosell, *The Surprising Work of God*, 127–47.

Harold John Ockenga

At the end of the evening, Ockenga rose to announce to the crowd the arrival of 1950. Having witnessed the remarkable events of the evening, including the four hundred young men and women whom he had just watched walk down the aisles at the close of Graham's message, Ockenga told the audience that he believed that they were all part of something much larger than a single service. "God has come to town," the brilliant pastor of Park Street Church and longtime student of spiritual awakenings was convinced. "The revival has broken in Boston" and if "New England can receive such a shaking of God under this stripling who like David of old went forth to meet the giant of the enemy, then we believe that God is ready to shake America to its foundations in revival."[27]

That New Years Eve service permanently changed the relationship between Ockenga and Graham. In Ockenga's eyes, the young "stripling" had emerged from that decisive service as a full-grown spiritual giant. Indeed, the subsequent revivals that broke-out in Boston and throughout New England early in 1950 further cemented their growing friendship and deepening trust. From 1950 until Ockenga's death in 1985, in fact, Graham and Ockenga remained in constant touch with one another and increasingly they joined hands on projects that they believed would further the vision in which they both so deeply believed: namely, the spread of the gospel around the globe; the renewal of the church through the clear and powerful preaching of the Word of God; the transformation of culture through Christian influence as "salt and light" in every segment of society; and the raising-up of a new generation of Christian leaders with "a burning love for Jesus."[28]

Among their most significant projects was the establishment of Gordon-Conwell Theological Seminary in 1969. "We have a need of new life from Christ in our nation," Ockenga once commented, and "that need first of all is intellectual." Unless "the Church can produce some thinkers who will lead us in positive channels our spiral of degradation will continue downward." Furthermore, he continued, "there is great need in the field of statesmanship."

27. The *Boston Post*, January 1, 1950, 15; Harold John Ockenga, "Boston Stirred by Revival," *United Evangelical Action*, January 15, 1950, 4, "Is America's Revival Breaking?" *United Evangelical Action*, July 1, 1950, and *The Great Awakening* (Boston: Fellowship, 1940). See also Rosell, *Surprising Work of God*, 127–47.

28. Garth M. Rosell, "The Ockenga Vision," in *Contact: The Ministry Magazine of Gordon-Conwell Theological Seminary*, Vol. 30, No. 1 (Summer 2000), 3–6, 10, 20–21; and *The Vision Continues: Centennial Papers of Gordon-Conwell Theological Seminary*, edited by Garth M. Rosell with an introduction by Robert E. Cooley, 1992.

Where are the political leaders "in high places of our nation," he asked, with "a knowledge of and high regard for the principles of the Word of God?" The need is "even more evident in the business world," he continued, where models of Christian integrity have become such a rarity. Most of all, he concluded, "there must be a new power in personal life. Unless this message of salvation which we hold to be the cardinal center of our Christian faith really does save individuals from sin, from sinful habits, from dishonesty, impurity and avarice, unless it keeps them in the midst of temptation, what good is it? Christians today are altogether too much like the pagan and heathen world both in actions and in life." What the church needs most at the present time and in the future "is saints, great Christians—Christ-loving men and women." Only out of such a company "can a new vision grow for the future of America." Our salvation is to be found in neither "a new economic-social order nor a political new deal" but rather in "Bible Christianity, with Christ the leader and eternity in view."[29]

Both Graham and Ockenga had long been convinced that the decision to locate the new seminary near Boston—the "Athens of America," with its dozens of educational institutions, scores of libraries, and potential access to the Boston Theological Institute—had been absolutely central to its future prospects and to the fulfillment of its founding vision. These intellectual, cultural, and spiritual resources would be essential, they were quite sure, if their lofty goals of spreading the gospel around the globe, of seeking the renewal of the church through the clear and powerful preaching of the Word, of working for the transformation of culture through Christian influence as "salt and light" were to become a reality. Throughout the history of the seminary, it is that founding vision that has drawn faculty, student body, administrators, and staff members to the seminary and that has enabled generations of faithful graduates to carry the good news of the gospel to a needy

29. Harold John Ockenga, "Christ for America," in *United Evangelical Action*, Vol. 2, No. 1 (May 4, 1943), 3-4, 6.

world. Without it, Ockenga and Graham believed, the seminary has neither the reason nor the right to exist.[30]

Board of Trustees

Earliest Known Photo of the Board of Trustees[31]

Faculty, students, administrators, and staff have not been alone in their commitment to the grand vision. Equally convinced

30. Harold John Ockenga, "Resurgent Evangelical Leadership," *Christianity Today* (October 10, 1960); "A New Evangelical Vision: The Leaders Speak Out," *Christian History* (Fall 2006).

31. Earliest known photo of the Gordon-Conwell Theological Seminary Board of Trustees (possibly taken in 1977 or 1978). From right to left around the table: Harold Lindsell (Chair), Harold John Ockenga (President), Curtiss C. Grove (Honorary Member), Unidentified, Isaac Green, George F. Bennett, Bill Pendleton, Head Blocked, Head Blocked, John G. Talcott, Jr., J. Duncan Brown, Allan C. Emery, Jr., Billy Graham, John Huffman, Mary French Rockefeller, Caroline Lynch Firestone, Head Blocked, H. Stuart Gray, Paul Toms, William C. Wood, Herbert Hess, Barbara Sweeney and Norman Klauder. Board members not pictured or unidentified: David W. Baker, G. Kurt Davidyan, Arthur S. DeMoss, Leighton Ford, Aaron E. Gast, John Pierce, John G. Talcott, Jr., Arthur C. Kenison, Robert J. Lamont, Lawrence H. Andreson, Michael E. Haynes, Walter R. Martin, Arthur N. Morris, Richard D. Phippin, and Phillip H. Smith. Special thanks to John Huffman and Bill Wood, longtime trustees, for their assistance in identifying their colleagues around the table.

have been the remarkable women and men who have agreed to serve without compensation on the seminary's board of trustees. While some members came to the new Gordon-Conwell Theological Seminary Board of Trustees by way of their previous service on either the Conwell Theological Seminary Board or the Gordon Divinity School Board, a number of strategic additions were made subsequently to provide the wisdom, insight and financial resources necessary to undergird the new seminary.

The Board of Trustees in 1983[32]

Outstanding pastors like Michael E. Haynes, Robert J. Lamont, John A. Huffman, Jr., Claude R. Alexander, Garth Bolinder, Harold

32. Gordon-Conwell Theological Seminary Board of Trustees in 1983. Front row: Morris, Viola, Gray, Ockenga, Davidyan, Talcott, Emery, Craft; Second row: Toms, Cooley (President), Hess, Andreson, Schultz, Rockefeller, Phippen, Haynes, Lyons; Third row: Armstrong, Huffman, Wood, Lamont, Potter, Pendleton, Bennett, Brown; Top row: Ford, Lindsell, Jacobi.

John Ockenga, Christopher A. Lyons, Peter G. James, Samuel Rodriguez, Jr., Richard P. Camp, David D. Swanson, Ken Shigematsu, and John H. Womack; gifted medical practitioners like William C. Wood, Joseph W. Viola, Shirley A. Redd, and Joyce A. Godwin; outstanding leaders in the financial world like George F. Bennett, Herbert P. Hess, Ivan C. Hinrichs, and Caleb Loring III; educators and teachers like Harold Lindsell, Linda Schultz Anderson, Stan D. Gaede, Charles W. Pollard, and Virginia M. Snoddy; business leaders like Richard A. Armstrong, Allan C. Emery, Jr., Thomas J. Colatosti, Kenneth H. Olsen, Thomas L. Phillips, Duncan Brown, Henderson Belk, H. Stuart Gray, Priscilla Hwang Lee, R. Bruce Bradley, and John Schoenherr; fine lawyers like Fred Potter, David M. Rogers, Sharon Fast Gustafson, and Christy Wilson III; gifted evangelists like Leighton Ford and Billy Graham; able accountants like Joel B. Aarsvold; and leaders of specialized ministries like Charles W. Colson, Diana Curren Bennett, Clyde W. Taylor, Anne Graham Lotz, and Joanna S. Mockler have enriched and guided the seminary across the years.

Harold Lindsell, Chair of the Board of Trustees, and President Ockenga
laying the cornerstone for Goddard Library

There is a special sense, of course, in which any Board of Trustees has a special duty and responsibility not only to appoint a president and ensure that the institution is financially sound but also to guarantee that the vision and mission of the seminary is preserved, protected and promoted through its various activities and programs. Since such duties and responsibilities do not happen automatically, as President Cooley recognized early in his administration, special care must be given to board training and development. Consequently, during the 1980s, with the assistance of a generous Lilly Endowment Board Development grant, a collection of talented and generous individuals were forged into an engaged, well-organized, and smoothly-functioning board.

President Ockenga and Trustee John Huffman[33]

33. John A. Huffman, a member of the Board of Trustees since the 1970s

At the very center of the initiative was the seminary's vision and mission—and special attention was given to understanding and promoting that vision and mission within board discussions and actions. In this connection, the founders of the seminary could not have been clearer as to what that vision and mission must continue to be: namely, the spread the gospel around the globe, the renewal of the church through the clear and powerful preaching of the Bible, the transformation of culture through Christian influence as "salt and light" and the training of new generations of Christian leaders with a thorough knowledge of the Scriptures, an understanding of culture, a love for the church, a missionary zeal, a passion for righteousness, a commitment to truth, a lifestyle of integrity and a burning love for Jesus. Of all the legacies of Brokaw's "greatest generation," the founders' vision was the most important of them all.

---

and its chairman from 2012 until 2018, has served the seminary in a variety of capacities from ministering as its "Pastor in Residence" and serving on its recent Presidential Search Committee to encouraging the appointment of J. Christy Wilson to its faculty.

CHAPTER III

Shaping a Faculty

All that is needed for a superior education is

Mark Hopkins on one end of a log and a student on the other

—JAMES A. GARFIELD

IN HIS ICONIC AND oft quoted comment, United States President James A. Garfield reduced the essentials of good education to three basic elements: a good teacher, a log and a willing student.[1] In our modern era with its increasingly comfy campuses, sports facilities, expanding administrations and emphasis on ease and convenience, such a comment sounds painfully quaint and somehow strangely out of place. Students no longer choose a school because of the faculty, a dean told me recently over lunch. Rather, they often select a school that is in a convenient location, that is flexible in its curricular requirements and that has an attractive financial aid program. With the advent of "online options," some even choose to opt out of residential education altogether.

---

1. *Frederick Rudolph, Mark Hopkins and the Log: Williams College, 1836–1872* (New Haven, CT: Yale University Press, 1956), Yale Historical Publications, Miscellany 63.

Clearly the dean has a point. However, his perspective is one that neither President Garfield, Mark Hopkins, nor the founders of our seminary would have shared. As President of Williams College and longtime Professor of Moral and Intellectual Philosophy on that campus, Mark Hopkins was convinced that the highest priority for any school was its duty to appoint morally upright and thoroughly trained men and women to the faculty since they are the primary reason that students choose to come. The important task of building a student's character, moral virtue, and discipline of mind, he was quite certain, requires nothing less than their regular, robust, tough-minded, face-to-face interactions with dedicated and well-trained teachers. That is precisely what Hopkins himself set out to accomplish through his own teaching and his students loved him for it. He was "a great teacher," President Garfield affirmed, and I would gladly have forfeited "all the buildings, apparatus and libraries" for the experience of simply studying with him.

Earliest Known Photograph of the Gordon-Conwell Theological Seminary Faculty[2]

2. Front Row (LtoR): Robert Fillinger, Glenn Barker, Burton Goddard, Roger Nicole, Harold John Ockenga, Stuart Barton Babbage; Second Row:

The founders of Gordon-Conwell Theological Seminary likewise understood that the appointment of a godly, well-trained faculty was the *sine qua non* for any theological seminary worthy of the name. Among the most important reasons that Billy Graham cited for merging Conwell and Gordon, as the reader may recall, was the absence of sufficient funding *and faculty* to sustain two evangelical seminaries that were located in the same part of the country. Well-trained and godly evangelical faculty members, it would seem, were still hard to find!

Seminary Faculty in 1978[3]

Stephen Mott, Meredith G. Kline, George Ensworth, William Lane, Gwyn Walters, W. Nigel Kerr; Third Row: David Scholer, Deane Kemper, Dick Camp, Richard Lovelace, Fred Prinzing, Ken Umenhofer, Addison H. Leitch; Top Row (Right): Unidentified. Not pictured: Lit-Sen Chang, James R. Hiles, Philip E. Hughes, Lloyd Kalland, Howard Keeley, J. Ramsey Michaels, Stephen M. Reynolds, Charles G. Schauffele and Daniel Weiss. This is the earliest known photograph of the newly combined Gordon-Conwell Theological Seminary faculty (undated but likely taken following the graduation ceremonies in 1971). With special appreciation to Meirwyn Walters, Jack and Robin Davis, Ken Swetland, and Doug Stuart for their help in dating the picture and identifying those in the photo.

3. Front row (left to right): J. Christy Wilson, David Scholer, Lloyd Kalland, Harold John Ockenga (President), Garth M. Rosell (Academic Dean), Dean Pedersen (Dean of Students), Robert Fillinger, Doug Stuart; Second row:

By the 1960s, however, the situation was beginning to change. Stuart Barton Babbage, as President of Conwell School of Theology, was determined to find, nurture and recruit the very best faculty candidates for the seminary.[4] The results of his efforts in Philadelphia are striking. Philip Edgecumbe Hughes, Richard Lovelace, Robert Sproul, James Hiles, and Wesley Roberts, to name but a few of his early recruits, not only had or soon would have earned doctorates but they had also begun to establish themselves as recognized scholars in their respective fields. Meanwhile, at Gordon Divinity School to the north, T. Leonard Lewis and Burton Goddard were hiring promising young scholars and established academics including Roger Nicole, Merrill Tenney, Gwyn Walters, Lit-Sen Chang, Glenn Barker, Addison Leitch, W. Nigel Kerr, Meredith Kline, Charles Schauffele, Ken Kantzer, George Ladd, and Lloyd Kalland. These exceptional scholars, combining piety and learning, began to attract a whole new cadre of students to the seminary.

Eldin Villafane, Elmer Smick, J. Ramsey Michaels, Dan Jessen, Jack Davis, Gwyn Walters, George Ensworth, Richard Peace; Third row: Dean Borgman, Andrew Lincoln, Bill Dyrness, Deane Kemper, Ken Swetland, Ray Pendleton, Richard Lovelace, Ken Umenhofer, Chuck Schauffele, Roger Nicole, Wes Roberts, Steve Mott, Carl Saylor.

4. The institutional archives of Gordon-Conwell Theological Seminary contain dozens of file folders for potential faculty appointees assembled by Babbage, drawn from around the world and containing *curricula vitae*, recommendation letters, supporting materials and additional correspondence. Babbage officially served as Executive Vice President from 1969 to 1971 (with Lloyd Kalland serving as Acting Dean during that time) and Vice President and Academic Dean from 1971 until 1973. William Nigel Kerr was appointed Acting Dean during 1973–1974 and Academic Dean from 1974 until 1978. Garth M. Rosell succeeded Dr. Kerr in 1978 and served as Vice President for Academic Affairs and Dean of the Seminary for nine years until returning to the classroom in 1987. Sidney DeWall served as Vice President for Academic Affairs and Dean of the Seminary from 1987 until 1992. Kenneth Swetland served as Acting Dean from 1992 to 1993 before being appointed Academic Dean in 1993, a post he filled until 1997 when his title became Dean of the Hamilton Campus, a change designed to reflect the growth of additional campus locations so as to include the Boston campus (Dean Alvin Padilla) and the Charlotte campus (Executive Dean Wayne E. Goodwin). The Jacksonville campus was overseen by the Academic Dean in Charlotte.

Gordon-Conwell Theological Seminary Faculty in the early 1980s[5]

Barbara Meissner, for example, graduated with the Master of Divinity degree from Gordon Divinity School in 1969 with the hope of serving as a missionary in Bolivia.[6] What drew her to Gordon Divinity School was most certainly not the promise of a comfy campus. Most of the married students, as she relates, lived either in "The Villa"—which was "in such a state of disrepair that it is to be demolished after Christmas"—or in the increasingly decrepit trailer park, lovingly known as "trailerville" by the students, next to "The Villa." Nor was it the "Hutter House"—the three-bedroom house, equipped with a dishwasher but no refrigerator, tables, chairs or dishes, in which Barbara lived along with five other single

5. Front row (left to right): J. Christy Wilson, T. David Gordon, Eldin Villafane, Aida Spencer, Jack Davis, George Ensworth; Second row: Jeff Niehaus, Gary Bekker, Richard Peace, Garth Rosell (Dean), Bob Fillinger, Ray Pendleton; Third row: Rick Lints, Greg Beale, Doug Stuart, Gary Pratico, Dan Jessen, Dean Borgman; Fourth row: David Wells, Steve Mott, Ken Swetland, Carl Saylor, Ken Umenhofer.

6. Barbara Meissner Kohl, "Beginnings," a delightful five-page typed manuscript that she sent to the author, February 17, 2018. For a faculty perspective on these days see Burton Goddard, "As I Remember the Seminary," his fourteen-page reflection written November 25, 1994. Copies in the Garth Mervin Rosell Papers (hereinafter the GMR Papers) housed at the seminary.

women. And it most certainly was not the promise of exceptional cuisine provided by the seminary, since she and her housemates did their own cooking to save a bit of money. Rather, what made the seminary experience so special for Barbara and students like her were the people—the wonderful friendships with other students, to be sure, but most especially the teachers. "When I arrived on campus the first night," she recalls, Dean Kerr met me and took me to the home of Professor and Mrs. Charles Schauffele where I was warmly welcomed and oriented to life at Gordon. Then Dr. and Mrs. Gwyn Walters "had us over for dinner and Mrs. Walters has been over several times to help us with the furnishing of our house."

Professor Lit-Sen Chang

Then, she continued, "I had dinner at Professor and Mrs. Lit-Sen Chang's home," both noted scholars from China. These are "just a few of the examples of how warmly and personally we have been treated," she continued, by what are "some of the great teachers in the world today. This personal interest is something I have never experienced on a university level before." During the day, from 7:45 a.m. until 3:30 p.m., she was in class with these same professors studying such subjects as church history, preaching, and Greek. Like James Garfield before her, she had occasion to sit as a willing student on one end of the metaphorical log while gifted teachers sat on the other—and it changed her life and prepared her for decades of effective ministry.

"Our standard," Harold John Ockenga had insisted at the founding of Fuller Theological Seminary in 1947, "will require every faculty member to be an accepted and recognized scholar in his own field" and we will "expect every student to be a graduate of an accepted college and to be screened to high spiritual and intellectual standards."[7]

Ockenga, who had himself earned both masters and doctoral degrees at the University of Pittsburgh, revisited these themes yet again on October 22, 1969 at his inauguration as President of Gordon-Conwell Theological Seminary. Our "teaching staff," he promised, will not only be "able to restate the Christian faith with relevance for our own day" but they will be able to relate the great truths of Scripture to every "aspect of our existence" from "education," "entertainment" and "the economic order" to "our family relationships" and the broader "cultural scene."[8]

7. Harold John Ockenga, "The Challenge to the Christian Culture of the West," an address at the opening convocation of Fuller Theological Seminary, October 1, 1947. Manuscript copy in the Harold John Ockenga Papers housed at Gordon-Conwell Theological Seminary. By contrast, as recently as 1940, Burton Goddard recalls, some three hundred Gordon College and Divinity School students were taught by "not more than ten" full-time faculty members, none of which "had an earned doctorate." See Burton L. Goddard, "As I Remember the Seminary," 1.

8. Harold John Ockenga, "Inaugural Acceptance Address," Installation as President of Gordon-Conwell Theological Seminary, October 22, 1969. Manuscript copy in the Harold John Ockenga Papers housed at Gordon-Conwell Theological Seminary.

Faculty and Trustees on a Spiritual Heritage Tour in 2003

The early leaders of the new seminary made good on that promise. The combined faculties of Conwell and Gordon, along with additional appointments made after the merger, formed an impressive community of piety and learning. Soon students, drawn by the compelling biblical vision that had shaped the seminary's founding and eager to study with Gordon-Conwell's distinguished faculty, began to make their way to New England. Ockenga had hoped that the seminary might eventually grow on the Hamilton campus to around seven hundred. It is unlikely, however, that he had anticipated that it would nearly reach that number by the end of his presidency a mere decade later. By the second half of the 1970s, in fact, one of the major problems facing the new dean who had arrived in 1978 was the burgeoning size of the seminary's student population. Indeed, it was not unusual in those days, given the expanding number of student applications, for the registration office to stop accepting new students as early as February for the Fall Semester since all available slots had already been filled.

The Old Chapel

Under Gordon-Conwell's second president, Robert E. Cooley, the seminary continued its pattern of growth both in student population (increasing from 694 to nearly a thousand) and in faculty strength (increasing from thirty-one to thirty-five).[9] A distinguished archaeologist himself, with deep roots in both the church and the academy, President Cooley not only consolidated the work of his predecessor but he also launched six important new initiatives designed to strengthen the faculty and to make the seminary even more attractive to prospective students: namely, the appointment of new faculty members; the establishment of a "distinguished chairs" program within the faculty; the strengthening of an ongoing faculty development program; the reorganization of faculty structures and procedures; the construction of a new academic center to provide space for classrooms, offices, and programs; and the raising of funds to undergird all that he and the board of trustees were seeking to accomplish.

At the top of the list was the appointment of much-needed new faculty members, including the first women to teach at the

9. Robert Cooley's served as president for sixteen years (1981–97). See "The Cooley Years," *Contact*, Vol. 26, No. 2 (Summer 1997).

seminary in such disciplines as New Testament, Classical and Ministry Studies, and Church History.[10] Special emphasis in the selection of new faculty, in addition to the seminary's traditional requirements for academic excellence, theological orthodoxy and effective teaching, was also placed on the need for greater racial and ethnic diversity within the faculty ranks, yielding some encouraging results. And the establishment of the president's innovative and strategically important program designed to enrich Gordon-Conwell's educational program with "distinguished chairs," provided the faculty with four new endowed chairs and one endowed professorship.[11] "I envision a quality faculty," Cooley had remarked at his installation, "men and women who represent some of the best minds, pastoral hearts and pioneering spirits in the Christian Church." Like President Ockenga before him, he was convinced that students would be drawn to study at the seminary by a quality faculty made up of professors "who challenge, who question, who listen and who care."[12]

10. The appointment of women in classical disciplines such as Biblical Studies and Church History, long staffed exclusively by men, was an enormous step forward for the seminary. Despite significant opposition from several quarters, Dr. Catherine Clark Kroeger was appointed a Ranked Adjunct Associate Professor of Classical and Ministry Studies in 1980; Dr. Aida Besancon Spencer was appointed Professor of New Testament in 1981; and Dr. Gwenfair Walters Adams was appointed Associate Professor of Church History in 1993. The high quality of their pioneering work opened the door for others so that women and men are now routinely considered for any and all faculty and administrative openings.

11. George Bennett, "A Tribute to President Robert E. Cooley," *Contact*, Vol. 26, No. 2 (Summer 1997), 2.

12. Remarks taken from President Cooley's inauguration address, reprinted in *Contact*, Vol. 12, No. 1 (Winter 1981–82), 1–5.

President Cooley and Dean Rosell

As a result of his "distinguished chair" program, dozens of prospective students, interested in learning how to preach, enrolled in the seminary primarily because Haddon Robinson had been appointed to the faculty as the Harold John Ockenga Distinguished Professor of Preaching. Scores of others, with interest in studying the world missionary movement, were drawn to the seminary by the appointment to another of the newly-established distinguished chairs of Peter Kuzmic, widely recognized as one of Eastern Europe's leading evangelical theologians and mission strategists. Those with interest in Historical Theology flocked to campus to study with David Wells who held the seminary's very first professorial chair, the Andrew Mutch Distinguished Professor of Historical and Systematic Theology. Still others with an interest in Biblical Studies travelled to New England to study with Scott Hafemann, Moises Silva, Eckhard Schnabel, or Walt Kaiser.

In addition to these distinguished chairs, other special positions were eventually added so that those interested in Religious Education, for example, were able to study with Linda Cannell and those with a calling to youth ministry came to learn from Dean Borgman. Those with particular interest in leadership came to study under Rodney L. Cooper, the Kenneth and Jean Hansen Professor of Discipleship and Leadership Development, and students with an interest in evangelism came to study with Robert E. Coleman, Distinguished Professor of Evangelism and Discipleship. Drawn to the seminary by such luminaries, students soon discovered a wealth of additional faculty resources on which they were able to draw. Like a great symphony, the Gordon-Conwell faculty successfully blended various instruments into a cohesive whole.

President Cooley's third key initiative was the strengthening of its faculty development program. "Wouldn't it be marvelous," President Cooley remarked to his Academic Dean as they travelled together on a 1983 Alumni Tour to Israel that he was leading, "if the whole faculty could share this experience with us?" After returning to campus, the dean contacted Dr. Robert Lynn at the Lilly Endowment to see if they might be willing to consider a proposal for a faculty development grant including funding for such a trip. Encouraged by Lilly's positive response, the dean along with a faculty committee began the lengthy process of preparing a proposal that included travel to Israel, individual grants for faculty research, and a generous fund overseen by the seminary to enable similar study tours every five or six years. For its part, the seminary promised to add to the fund annually so that similar faculty experience might be continued.

The first part of Lilly's generous grant made possible the fourteen-day study tour of Israel in January of 1985 by sixty-four faculty members along with spouses and even some of their children. "Israel is a land that touches on each of our disciplines," wrote Professor Richard Peace in his evaluation of the program. "The opportunity to view that land through the lens of each of these disciplines was rewarding and broadening." The "faculty has imparted various dimensions of this experience with every segment of the Seminary community" remarked Gary Pratico, a Professor of Old Testament who led the educational program with President Cooley. "Many lectures of the new semester reflect the impressions of this unique study experience. Scholarship, from research to writing has been impacted. A new sense of collegiality has emerged. In a very real sense, a new spirit is apparent on the Seminary campus." [13]

Encouraged by the overwhelming success of the Israel trip and enabled by the generosity of the Lilly Endowment, Dean Ken Swetland organized a subsequent Faculty Study Tour of Turkey and Greece several years later—an experience, as had been the case in Israel earlier, that not only informed and inspired the faculty but also built new friendships and deepened its shared sense of community. Several years later, Dean Barry Corey drew yet again on the fund to underwrite a Spiritual Heritage Tour of New England for the nearly one-hundred seminary faculty and trustees who travelled together on two large tour busses to visit sites throughout the New England region. [14] Taken together, as one member of the faculty phrased it, "these unique experiences did more to build a sense of community within the faculty as anything the seminary has ever done."

A fourth initiative focused on the reorganization of faculty structures and processes. The early years of many institutions, including seminaries like Gordon-Conwell, seem inevitably to be structured a bit like "Mom and Pop" stores. With growth and increasing complexity, however, comes the need for clear policies,

13. Taken from a report titled "Israel Study Trip 'surpassed even the lofty expectations of faculty,'" in *Hilltop*, an in-house publication of Gordon-Conwell Theological Seminary, 1985.

14. Garth M. Rosell, *Exploring New England's Spiritual Heritage: Seven Daytrips for Contemporary Pilgrims* (Peabody, MA: Hendrickson, 2019) and "Faculty Spiritual Heritage Tour Notebook," August 27–28, 2003, copy in the GMR Papers housed at the seminary.

written procedures, and the development of organizational structures. As a trained archaeologist, President Cooley brought with him an understanding of how systems work and an interest in structural balance and integrity. Consequently, among his earliest initiatives as president were the writing and adoption of an institutional "Mission Statement," the establishment of a development program for the Board of Trustees; and a thorough review of institutional policies, procedures, and organizational structures. With respect to the faculty, he called for a revision of its "Faculty Handbook," a process that included annual updates and approvals by vote of both faculty and board, and a review of its organizational structures, its policies, and its procedures. As a result of those reviews, among other changes, were the adoption of three faculty divisions to replace the old departmental structure, the establishment of the Faculty Personnel Policies Committee to replace the old Faculty Senate and the significant reduction in the number of faculty committees to which each faculty member was annually assigned. [15] These changes, for the most part, reduced the heavy administrative load carried by faculty members and freed significantly more time for the important work of teaching, research and service.

15. A full set of *Faculty Minutes*, covering the years from June 1970 through September 11, 1992 are available in two large black notebooks in the Goddard Library on the Hamilton Campus, Gordon-Conwell Theological Seminary. These provide, in detail, the many changes that were adopted during the early years of the seminary. These curricular offerings were further enhanced through the use of visiting professor, adjuncts, and special lecture series.

The fifth initiative was the construction of five new buildings on the Hamilton campus: the chapel, three married student apartments with over two hundred new units, and the academic center. The academic center, funded largely from a generous gift from the Pew Charitable Trusts, provided much needed classrooms, faculty offices, and program spaces. And a sixth initiative, designed to raise much-needed funds to undergird the other initiatives and to strengthen the seminary's educational mission, included two successful capital campaigns (1987–91; 1991–95) that raised a total of over sixty-five million dollars and that increased the seminary's endowment funds from less than a million dollars to more than twenty-six and its total assets (debt-free) to nearly fifty-seven million.[16]

Other important initiatives by Cooley's four successors in the office of president, as we will have occasion to see, added their own special texture and shape to faculty life and work. However, there is a sense in which the "founders" and "builders" presidencies of Ockenga and Cooley, spanning nearly three decades between 1969 and 1997, set many of the educational trajectories and established many of the organizational structures that have continued to order faculty life throughout its history.

Three central themes emerge from the scores of recorded oral history interviews that were conducted with faculty members who were part of the Gordon-Conwell Theological Seminary community during those first three decades.[17] The first, and perhaps most significant, was the faculty's deep commitment to the seminary's mission. Its six central articles, the details of which we will have occasion to explore in a later chapter, were understood, practiced and affirmed in the strongest possible terms. Despite lively debate on scores of secondary issues—and there seemed to be an abundance of those judging by the constant stream of campus forums

16. "The Cooley Years," *Contact*, Vol.26, No. 2 (Summer 1997), 2, 4–5.

17. The author's Oral History Project, conducted with thirty-four individuals between 2012 and 2018, fill nearly one hundred tapes with reflections, remembrances and insights relating to the history of the seminary. They are now part of the GMR Papers housed at the seminary.

such as the packed-out "grapple in the chapel" and "Almost 60 Minutes"—the faculty had clearly closed ranks around a set of core theological beliefs and practices on which they were passionately united—from the authority of the Bible and the centrality of Christ's atoning work on the cross to the importance of the original languages and the need for excellence in the teaching of the classical disciplines.

"Almost 60 Minutes" Forum in 1978[18]

A second discovery reflected in the interviews was how fondly those early faculty members recalled the lively debates that seemed to break out with some regularity at the faculty meetings—from Roger Nicole's determined attempts to thwart a faculty vote to reduce the number of theology requirements in the Master of Divinity degree from four to three to the lengthy discussions relating to whether or not the faculty should approve a new Doctor of Ministry degree program—as a deeply-engaged, well-trained, and strong-spirited faculty sought under the guidance of the Holy Spirit to arrive at worthy and God-honoring decisions. The air on

18. "Almost 60 Minutes" forum with (left to right) Pete James (Student Association President), David Scholer (NT), Roger Nicole (Theology), Ramsey Michaels (NT) and Jack Davis (Theology).

campus those days—in hallways and classrooms—fairly crackled and buzzed with theological discussion and lively debate. It was an exciting time to be at the seminary and it continued to attract students from around the globe who seemed anxious to get in on the action.

Roger Nicole, Jim Packer, and Jeannette Scholer

Undergirding the ferment, as a third characteristic of the interviews, was the strong sense of faculty community that they reflected. Despite their heated debates, faculty members seemed to really like and respect each other and they certainly enjoyed being together. Overnight faculty retreats, whether at the Salvation Army Campground in Sharon, Massachusetts or the Advent Christian Campground in Alton Bay, New Hampshire, always involved times for recreation at the volleyball net or on the basketball court, time for good conversations on the hiking trails and times of joyous singing with Bob Dvorak in the lead and often with Doug Stuart at the piano. The faculty also gathered annually for Christmas parties at the Rosell home in Wenham (sometimes including the singing of the "Hallelujah Chorus" from Handel's

Messiah, in full harmony no less!), for times of prayer, for pancake breakfasts, and for the regular luncheon gatherings that faculty and spouses enjoyed at the Easterly (overlooking Bass Rocks in Gloucester) where "awards" were always handed out, sometimes accompanied by a bit of doggerel, for faculty achievements that were both real and imagined.

On occasion, a comfortable coach would be hired to take faculty and spouses to the Boston Symphony, with Richard Lovelace providing a preparatory musical lecture *en route* into town and a Boston restaurant providing dessert and conversation before the faculty re-boarded the coach for its trip back to campus. On one occasion, the faculty even tried its hand at deep-sea fishing with a morning aboard a big Gloucester fishing boat followed by an afternoon faculty family picnic at Christy Wilson's beautiful rented home overlooking the Anisquam River on Cape Ann. Since Harold John Ockenga had caught the largest fish taken that morning, his huge Cod was cooked over the coals (without his permission some recall) and served to the nearly one hundred hungry and grateful attendees.

Gordon Fee in Lecture Hall I

Faculty gatherings, of course, were not all social in nature. At the invitation of the dean and faculty at Union Theological Seminary in New York City, members of the Gordon-Conwell faculty travelled to the UTS campus for several days of evangelical and liberal dialog on several important theological issues. On another occasion, the faculty of Holy Cross Greek Orthodox Seminary and Gordon-Conwell Theological Seminary held a conference on preaching that proved to be both interesting and enlightening. On yet another occasion, members of the seminary faculty joined with several other faculties for a two-week "Globalization in Theological Education" immersion experience in the subcontinent of India sponsored by the Association of Theological Schools and funded by a generous grant. And on yet another occasion, members of the faculty gathered with faculty members from four other seminaries for the Lilly Endowment-funded Lexington Seminar—a week of intensive discussions on theological teaching and learning held at the historic Asticou Inn in Northeast Harbor, Maine.

These and other similar events helped to strengthen a sense of community within the faculty and they went a long way toward encouraging the kind of deep friendship and trust among colleagues that not only made teaching for many at Gordon-Conwell a genuine delight but that also provided a foundation of trust when difficult decisions were faced and opinions were divided. Most especially, they helped to undergird the central faculty task of teaching the students whom God had called to study and learn here in New England.

All of which, of course, brings us back to the teacher and the student on the log! Whether sitting across from one student in their faculty office or looking out on a hundred students in Lecture Hall I, members of the seminary's faculty—in that unique bond that exists between teacher and learner—became for many of our students and eventual graduates not only the reason they came to Gordon-Conwell Theological Seminary in the first place but it was also a significant reason that they remained on our campus until graduation. Those special bonds with particular faculty members, for so many of the seminary graduates, were among the most enduring memories of their seminary experience.

Betty Lee and Richard Lovelace

CHAPTER IV

Attracting a Student Body

The world does not need sermons; it needs a message. You can go to
seminary and learn how to preach sermons, but you will have to go
to God to get messages.[1]

—OSWALD J. SMITH

"THE MIND IS NOT a vessel to be filled," wrote the Greek philoso-
pher Plutarch nearly two millennia ago, "but a fire to be kindled."[2]
The old teacher's words are as relevant for theological students
and professors today as they were for Plutarch's young student
Nicander who in the first century was planning to take up the serious study of philosophy. Indeed, it would be well for contemporary students to read this ancient essay "On Listening to Lectures"
before launching into their own theological studies and it might

1. Quotation by Oswald J. Smith is taken from "Seminary Quotes," www.
azquotes.com

2. Plutarch and Frank Cole Babbitt, *Plutarch, Moralia I,* "On Listening to
Lectures" (Cambridge: Harvard University Press, 1927), 256–57. Translated
"For the Mind does not require filling like a bottle, but rather, like wood, it
only requires kindling to create in it an impulse to think independently and an
ardent desire for the truth."

be helpful for faculty members to read Plutarch's essay since it provides a valuable reminder that the teacher's primary task is not so much to "fill the bottle" with knowledge as it is to help ignite in their students a thirst for truth, a passion for learning, and a hunger for divine wisdom. Indeed, it is God who calls both teachers and learners to their important tasks; it is God who enables them to teach and learn; and it is God, through his revelation in the Bible and his glorious creation, who provides the message that teachers and students alike must embrace, embody, and proclaim.

The seminary's founding faculty could not have agreed more. "The seminary exists to serve the students and not to serve the faculty," remarked professor Stephen Charles Mott as the faculty gathered for its annual retreat at the start of the 1974/1975 academic year. "God has given us a commission to prepare men and women to serve in the church and in the world," Dean William Nigel Kerr reminded his colleagues, and "God alone can fit us for the fulfillment of the charge." If we are to properly instruct and inspire our students, we must learn to love God above all else and we must learn to love our students. "Our great task is to depend on God, who gives life, hope, and power to those who will serve Him." [3]

---

3. William Nigel Kerr, "Faculty Gathers for Retreat," *The Gordon-Conwell Contact*, Fall Report (1974), Vol. V, No. 1, 6. The retreat was held at Cushing Hall in Wenham, a home for retired Sisters of Notre Dame. Among the highlights was the singing of "Guide Me, O Thou Great Jehovah" and "Praise the Savior, Yet who know Him," two hymns that had been requested by the sisters.

Faculty and Trustee Retreat [4]

As the faculty and trustees gathered in the early autumn of 1974, as was their annual practice since the seminary's founding, they were well aware that student enrollment at the seminary was rapidly increasing. The 279 students who enrolled for the Fall Semester of 1969 had grown to 320 by the following academic year, drawn from thirty-five different states and eleven nations.[5] By the Fall Semester of 1971 it had risen another 27%. "Enrollment; A New Record" announced the headline in the seminary's *Contact* magazine.[6] By 1972, it had climbed to yet another record with 466 students. "Student Enrollment Up: A New Profile," reported *Contact*. "They fill the chapel, they flood the cafeteria" and "they pack those first-year Master of Divinity required courses. So, of course, registration was a stand-in-line process for everyone—at the offices of the cashier, the professors, the Registrar and in the halls."

4. Held at "Hillwinds," the Ockenga's summer home in New Hampshire, in 1978.

5. *GCTS Catalog for 1970–1971*

6. *Gordon-Conwell Theological Seminary Contact* (Winter 1971), Vol. 2, No. 1, 7. The growth was from 320 to 407 full-time students.

Noting that the seminary's growth was already ahead of projections, Douglas K. Stuart the Director of Registration "pointed out that the present student body was 14% larger" than it had been the previous year.[7]

Billy Graham Speaking in Chapel

By 1973, in a *Contact* article titled "Careful Control Allows Enrollment to Reach 500," the administration announced that applications were continuing to exceed projections.[8] By 1974, in fact, enrollment had increased to 540. By 1975 it had grown to 575. By 1976 it was 620, by 1978 student enrollment was 641 and by 1980 it had increased to a whopping 694![9]

"In a growing school," wrote Doug Stuart, "it is not surprising that each year a new record is set for size." "How does it happen that we have so many students? The biggest single factor," Stuart was convinced, "is undoubtedly the quality of the alumni that the school has produced in the past. It is very clear to those of us who work in admissions that past graduates of our school are not only serving as models for ministry to students considering seminary training, but also are actively recruiting and directing students our

7. *Gordon-Conwell Theological Seminary Contact* (Fall 1972), Vol. 3, No. 1, 4–5.

8. *Gordon-Conwell Theological Seminary Contact* (Summer 1973), Vol. 3, No. 4, 3.

9. Among the reasons for the seminary's rapid early growth was the Jesus People Movement. See Larry Eskridge, *God's Forever Family: The Jesus People Movement in America* (New York: Oxford University Press, 2013).

way. One result is that the Seminary received just slightly under 500 applications asking for admission this year, of which 222 actually became students."[10]

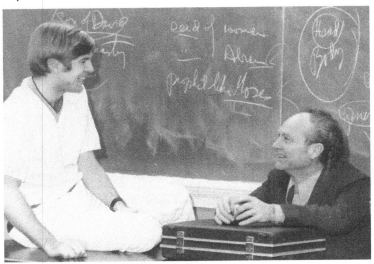

Professor Meredith Kline after Class

Although growth in student enrollment was seen by most as a great blessing, it did expose some important emerging problems. Notable among these was the growing gap between the numbers of students who were coming to the seminary and the number of faculty members who were responsible to teach them. "We do have a faculty-student ratio that comes very close to the brink of the outer limits set for accreditation," reported Stuart in his 1975 article. With a full-time faculty of twenty-four and a student population of nearly six hundred, there are already "far too many large classes" and it is becoming increasingly difficult to deliver "the personal kind of education" that students have come to Gordon-Conwell to find.[11]

10. Douglas K. Stuart, "A Profile of the Seminary with Commentary: 1975–76," *Gordon-Conwell Theological Seminary Contact* (Fall 1975), Vol. 6, No. 1, 2–3.

11. Stuart, "A Profile," 2–3.

Professor Wesley Roberts with Students

To address the faculty/student ratio problem, the seminary began to make much-needed additions to the faculty. Stephen Charles Mott, in Social Ethics, was added in 1970. Elmer Smick and Doug Stuart, in Biblical Studies, were added in 1971. Wesley Roberts, in Church History and Black Studies, was added in 1972 along with the appointment of Kenneth Swetland as Director of the Alumni Office and Robert Dvorak to replace the retiring Burton Goddard as Director of the Library. Eric Lemmon was added to the theology department in 1973 and Carlyle Saylor was appointed as Director of Field Education in 1974. Gordon Fee and Andrew Lincoln, both in New Testament, were added in 1975 as were Christy Wilson in Missions, Jack Davis in Theology and Ray Pendleton in Counseling and Pastoral Care. Over the next decade, seven more appointments were made to the faculty: Garth M. Rosell as Academic Dean and Professor of Church History, David Wells in Theology, Jeffrey Niehaus in Old Testament, Aida Spencer in New Testament, Gary Pratico in Old Testament, T. David Gordon in New Testament, Greg Beale in Biblical Studies and Richard Lints in Theology. By 1985, with a student enrollment of 669, the seminary faculty had twenty-nine regular classroom professors with rank, five administrators or program directors who also taught some courses, eleven adjuncts on the Hamilton campus and seventeen on the Boston campus plus six Greek, Hebrew, and Latin Teaching Fellows.[12]

Francis Schaffer Interacts with Students

The make up of the student body, which had grown to 669 by 1985, was also reflecting some changing patterns.[13] Significant increases in the number of women, minorities, internationals and married students had occurred over the seminary's first decade and a half.[14] Summer School enrollment had risen from seventy-

12. Gordon-Conwell Theological Seminary, Accreditation Self-Study, 1985, 17.

13. GCTS, Accreditation Self-Study, 1985, 28–45.

14. As reported in the "Student Chapter" of the Accreditation Self-Study for 1985, 28–44. The number of married students had grown by 44%, the number of women in degree programs had increased from seventy-four to 120, and the number of minority and international students had grown to forty. The average age of the students was reported as 30.2 years.

seven students in 1974 to 235 students in 1984. Cross registrations of Gordon-Conwell students into Boston Theological Institute member schools grown from forty-three in 1973 to 102 in 1984 and cross registrations from BTI member schools into Gordon-Conwell classes had increased from three in 1973 to thirty in 1984.[15] The Doctor of Ministry degree program, by its fourth year in 1985, had grown to forty students.[16] And enrollment in the Center for Urban Ministerial Education in Boston (CUME), having been launched in 1976 and offering in-service courses in English, Spanish, French, and Portuguese for urban pastors and church leaders in the greater Boston area, had grown from thirty students in 1976 to 177 students by 1983.[17] Forty-two states, thirteen nations, and forty different denominations were represented on the seminary's two campus settings by 1985.[18]

Some of the Seminary's Outstanding Staff[19]

15. For the full report see Accreditation Self-Study for 1985, 104–5.

16. For the full report see Accreditation Self-Study for 1985, 53–54.

17. For the full report see Accreditation Self-Study for 1985, 55–57.

18. Accreditation Self-Study for 1985, 28.

19. From left to right: Virginia Steadman, Mildred Passler, Jeanie Sweet, Esther Flewelling, Unidentified, Unidentified, Mavis Cooter, Louise Cary.

Trustees Paul Toms, Richard Phippin, Mary Rockefeller, and Allan Emery

To address the extra-curricular needs of the growing student body, the seminary appointed Richard Camp as its first Dean of Students in the Fall Semester of 1970. Having served as pastor of the South Shore Baptist Church in Hingham, Massachusetts, Dick helped to shape an office that was responsible for overseeing financial assistance, student services, housing, employment, counseling, placement, international student concerns, student government functions, women's concerns, ethnic minority concerns, spiritual life, advisement, discipline, seminary spouses concerns, denominational concerns, and orientation. "I see my work," remarked Camp, as helping the students while they are here in every area of their lives "apart from academics." [20] After completing three outstanding years as Dean of Students, Dick left the seminary in 1974 to take up his new responsibilities as the Protestant Chaplain at the

---

Special thanks to Lurline (Mears) Umenhofer for her help in identifying those pictured in the photo.

20. Gordon-Conwell *Contact* (October 1970), Vol. 1, No. 1, 2; and Accreditation Self-Study for 1985, 29–45.

United States Military Academy at West Point. Camp subsequently served as a trustee of the seminary.

Bradley, Virjean, Richard, and Kristen Camp[21]

In the Fall of 1976, to the great delight of the entire campus, Dean W. Pedersen was appointed as the new Dean of Students. Having served as School Minister and member of the teaching faculty at the Peddie School in Hightstown, New Jersey from 1970 to 1976, after service in Viet Nam as a Navy Chaplain, "double Dean," as he was affectionately known, ministered to the seminary students with grace and uncommon skill for the next twelve years. Although two remarkable men, Ken Swetland and Scott Gibson preceded Camp and Pedersen and three remarkable women, Lita Schlueter, Michelle Williams, and Jana Holiday, subsequently succeeded him in that important office, Dean Pedersen's work was pivotal in providing shape and clear direction for student ministries on campus.[22]

21. Gordon-Conwell *Contact* (Fall 1973), Vol. 4, No. 1, 8. Dr. Fred Prinzing, Assistant Professor of Ministry and Director of Field Education, replaced Camp briefly before the appointment in 1976 of Dean Pedersen. Gordon-Conwell *Contact* (Winter 1974), Vol. 4, No. 2, 2.

22. Gordon-Conwell *Contact* (Fall 1976), Vol. 7, No. 1, 3.

Dean Pedersen

Under the guidance of the Dean of Students, a variety of services and ministries were increasingly sharpened to enhance the campus experience for students—from housing and financial aid to spiritual life and placement. In addition, the Women's Council, established in 1928, has throughout its distinguished history taken a special interest in the welfare of students—raising thousands of dollars for student scholarships and providing opportunities for fellowship, service, and inspiration.[23] The spiritual, academic, and practical needs of students have been further enhanced through access to the seminary's regular chapel services and through the work of the seminary's various counseling programs, the Mentored

23. For the story of The Women's Council see "The Women's Council Celebrates 80 Years of Service," a video produced in 2008.

Ministry Program, the Pierce Center for Disciple-Building, the Center for the Development of Evangelical Leadership, the Center for the Study of Global Christianity, the Institute for the Study of the Black Christian Experience, the Center for World Missions, the Minister in Residence program, the various lecture series, the Haddon Robinson Center for Preaching, the Shoemaker Center for Church Renewal, the Robert C. Cooley Center for the Study of Early Christianity, the Mockler Center for Marketplace Ministries and through seminary publications like *Contact Magazine*, the *Ministry List, InCommunity, The Hilltop*, and the *Africanus Journal*.[24]

This growing network of support programs and personal friendships greatly strengthened the already deep bonds that often develop between individual students and their favorite faculty members. Indeed, the hours of conversation, prayer, and fellowship that the teaching faculty have traditionally spent with individual students have not only helped them to sort out issues of vocational call, theological convictions, and ethical concerns during their years on campus but they have also led to relationships that have continued long after a student has received their degree.

Doug Stuart and Nigel Kerr talk with Prospective Students

24. Information on all of these varied ministries can be found on the seminary's website.

Whether sitting with others in a seminar room, meeting one-on-one in the hallway, or gathering in faculty homes, students have been encouraged by the seminary's faculty to think, analyze, interpret, write, and speak clearly and they have been urged, as master-level students, to master as fully as possible the "content" of the various disciplines to which they are being exposed within the theological curriculum. Mastery of the basic "stuff" of each field has always been considered an essential foundation for theological education. Plutarch may have been right about the priority of kindling a fire rather than simply filling a bottle, but faculty members at Gordon-Conwell Theological Seminary have rarely been satisfied with anything less than a commitment to both.

"The proof," so to speak, "has been in the pudding" since so many of the seminary's more than 10,000 graduates have carried both the "content" and the "fire" into their various venues and callings. Having been trained and inspired while students here on campus, literally hundreds of graduates have gone from the seminary to make a significant difference throughout the world.

Professor William Nigel Kerr

Some, of course, are now quite famous. Timothy J. Keller, whose writings and remarkable ministry at Redeemer Presbyterian Church in New York City have made his name familiar to many, completed his basic theological training here at the seminary (MDiv'75). Barbara Ernst Prey, considered "one of America's most gifted watercolorists" and whose paintings hang in some of the world's most prestigious galleries, was for a time a student here at the seminary. Ben Witherington III, who completed the Master of Divinity degree in 1977 before earning a PhD degree at the University of Durham, has established himself as one of the world's leading New Testament scholars. Douglas Birdsall, who completed his Master of Divinity in 1979, is perhaps best known for his work as the Executive Chairman of the Lausanne Committee for World Evangelization. Michael Ford, the oldest of President Gerald and Betty Ford's four children, completed the Master of Divinity degree here at Gordon-Conwell in 1977 and went on to minister as a chaplain and pastor. Scott M. Gibson, who for many years served as the Haddon W. Robinson Professor of Preaching and Ministry and Director of the Haddon W. Robinson Center for Preaching at Gordon-Conwell, was recently appointed the David E. Garland Chair of Preaching and Director of the PhD Program in Preaching at Baylor University's Truett Seminary. Kimberly and Scott Hahn, gifted and well-known authors, both graduated from the seminary in 1982. James Banks, a gifted pastor who graduated with the Doctor of Ministry degree in 2007, has broadened the impact of his ministry through his well-known publications on prayer. Scott W. Sunquist, who recently served as Dean and Professor of World Christianity in the School of Intercultural Studies at Fuller Theological Seminary, was appointed in 2019 as Gordon-Conwell's seventh president. Timothy Tennent, who with his wife Julie graduated in 1984 and who later served on the faculty of Gordon-Conwell, now serves as President of Asbury Theological Seminary. Other notable graduates—from Gordon P. Hugenberger (MDiv'74), Rikk Watts (MDiv'87), and John Jefferson Davis (MDiv'72) to Mark Dever (MDiv'86), Elisabeth Ostling (MASF'17), and Jerry Camery-Hoggatt (MTS'78)—could be added to a rapidly growing list of those who through their example have helped to introduce a North American seminary to a much wider audience.

Dr. Peter Kuzmic with Global Leadership Seminar students in Bosnia[25]

Thousands of additional graduates, equally notable but perhaps less well known, have made use of their seminary training in their work as pastors, teachers, medical personnel, chaplains, missionaries, accountants, biologists, business administrators, musicians, counselors, computer programmers, dentists, contractors, editors, engineers, marketers, journalists, lawyers, financial analysts, librarians, parachurch directors, publishers, photographers, psychologists, researchers, stockbrokers, youth leaders, artists, entrepreneurs, plumbers, truck drivers, poets, nurses, social

25. Dr. Peter Kuzmic, Paul E. and Era B. Toms Distinguished Professor of World Missions and European Studies, with a group of senior Master of Divinity students on the annual "Global Leadership Seminar" in a bombed out city in Bosnia: (left to right: Stephen Lane, Dale Tadlock [a Bulgarian graduate student of Evangelical Theological Seminary in Osijek], John Dawson, Professor Kuzmic, Matthew Beatty, James Teall, Moonbong Yang, Mary Lewis and Joannah Cook). Photo taken by Karmelo and provided courtesy of Professor Kuzmic.

workers, administrators, merchants, presidents, deans, homemakers, electricians, technicians, and dozens of additional godly callings. Some like Adrian Weimer, Heather Maw Curtis, Brandon Bayne, Chad Gunoe, Mark Briesmaster, George and Anne Harper, Andrew Kloes, Tom and Donna Petter, Aaron Gies, Helen Brouillette, Chris Chun, Jennifer Creamer, Jim Critchlow, Ed Keazirian, Jim Peterson, Bob Pazmino, Todd Pokrifka, Carol Kaminski, Martin Dotterweich, Christine Cos, Mark Chapman, Josh Kercsmar, Allen Yeh, Kent Yinger, Laura Miguelez Quay, Kristina LaCelle-Peterson, Patricia Hill-Ziegler, David Eastman, Kathy Dunderdale, Andrew Drenas, Linford Fisher, Chris Armstrong, Efrain Agosto, David Aiken, Curtis Evans, Esther Bruland, Margaret Kim, Kathryn Long, Diana Butler Bass, Andrea Turpin, Sean McDonough, and a host of others have completed first-rate doctoral programs and most are now actively engaged in teaching and writing at a variety of universities, colleges, seminaries, Bible schools, and other educational institutions around the world.

Hundreds of others like Bill Boylan, Nick Granitsas, Lou Mitchell, Mark Acuff, Rachel Stahle, Kevin Adams, Pete Ballentine, Tom Petter, Pete and Andrew James, Claude Alexander, David Rockness, Ken Shigematsu, John Wood, and Tim Ziegenhals have served or are serving as faithful pastors for spiritual flocks around the world. Still others like David Teague, Patrick Lowthian, and Douglas McCready are fulfilling their callings as chaplains, counselors or consultants. Still others like Efrain Agosto, David Currie, Katherine Horvath, Al Padilla, Pedro Govantes, Scott Poblenz, and Eugene Heacock are fulfilling their callings as gifted administrators. Hundreds more like Andrew Kaiser, Doug Birdsall, Paul Martindale, Kevin Rall, Rich Stuebing, Paul Sydnor, Bob Vetter, and Darius Brycko have sensed God's call to missionary service in a variety of venues around the world. These servants of God—and hundreds more who are represented by them, have brought and continue to bring great credit to the work of the seminary through their humble, faithful and godly service to the Lord of Lords and the King of Kings.

CHAPTER V

Designing a Curriculum

It is easier to move a cemetery than to change a curriculum[1]

—WOODROW WILSON

AMERICA'S OLDEST PROTESTANT THEOLOGICAL seminary was founded in 1807 at Andover, Massachusetts. With its original campus located only about twenty miles from property that would become—a century and a half later—the main campus of Gordon-Conwell Theological Seminary, Andover Theological Seminary officially opened its doors to students in 1808. With its now familiar three-year curriculum, Andover quickly became the recognized model for how American theological education should be done.[2]

1. Taken from www.azquotes.com

2. Leonard Woods, *History of the Andover Theological Seminary* (Boston: James R. Osgood and Co., 1885); Glenn T. Miller, *Piety and Intellect: The Aims and Purposes of Ante-Bellum Theological Education* (Atlanta: Scholars Press, 1990); William C. Ringenberg, *The Christian College* (Grand Rapids: Eerdmans, 1984); Heather F. Day, *Protestant Theological Education in America: A Bibliography* (Lanham, MD: Scarecrow Press, 1985); and Margaret Lamberts Bendroth, *A School of the Church: Andover Newton Across Two Centuries* (Grand Rapids: Eerdmans Publishing Co., 2008). "The Andover model," Bendroth writes, was "soon the standard form for theological education in every denomination across the country."

70

From a curricular standpoint, the Andover model was revolutionary. Not only were students expected to enter seminary with "a certificate of good character" and "a college degree" already in hand, but during their three years of study they were also expected to demonstrate a mastery of ecclesiastical history, Christian theology, preaching, apologetics, ethics, philosophy, and the Scriptures in their original languages. The first year students, along with an introduction to theology, normally focused their studies on the Bible, "including Hebrew grammar and hermeneutics" along with "New Testament Greek and exegesis of the four Gospels." The second year, or middler, students "met five days a week for instruction in theology, supplemented by more New Testament exegesis and topical lectures in 'sacred literature.'" With those foundations in hand, the third year students focused their final year on church history and preaching along with additional work in Hebrew and Greek exegesis. "At the end of each school year, students stood for public examinations by the faculty" to demonstrate their mastery of the entire curriculum. "Study at Andover," as historian Margaret Lamberts Bendroth insightfully phrased it, "was not for the faint of heart."

Nor was the Andover curriculum for the lazy or slothful! Each day began with worship at 7:00 a.m. and continued until 9:00 p.m. with classes, study, recitation, prayer, manual labor, and meals. Even Sundays, following worship, were given to study, recitation, reading, and prayer. On Wednesday evenings, President Leonard Woods "led them for an hour of prayer and instruction on topics conducive of personal piety." Tuition and board, thanks to their generous endowment, was essentially free although students were expected to do regular manual labor, growing food for their meals, and to gather sufficient wood to heat their rooms, the classroom and the dining hall.

The seminary faculty for their part—including Eliphalet Pearson, Leonard Woods, Edward Dorr Griffin, Moses Stuart, and Edward Robinson—were expected to lecture twice daily and to serve as spiritual guides watching "over their pupils' health and morals with 'paternal solicitude.'"[3]

What is surprising, when comparing early Andover with many seminaries today, is how similar they are in their curricular design. While such matters as the daily schedule, the calendar year, the cost of tuition, the sequencing of courses, and the summative exams may have changed dramatically over the past two-hundred years, the core curricular requirements seem to have remained remarkably consistent. Subjects such as Systematic Theology, Church History, Old and New Testament, Hermeneutics, Preaching, Apologetics, Ethics, and the Biblical Languages are as much a part of contemporary seminary life as they were in the early nineteenth century. Indeed, the similarities between the curricular structure in early Andover and the contemporary curricular structure on the various campuses of Gordon-Conwell Theological Seminary are striking. Minor differences exist, of course—such as the addition of such required courses as "Clinical Pastoral Training" and the "Administration of Christian Education"—yet in its essential core, the old Andover seminary model has remained largely intact.[4]

Not everyone has been sanguine, of course, about the persistence of such remarkable continuity. Convinced that the old Andover model needs a complete updating and overhaul—or at least a significant tweaking—some members of Gordon-Conwell's faculty, administration, and board have called from time to time for "curricular reform." The "Faculty Minutes," when read chronologically over the course of the seminary's history, reflect literally dozens of lively and sometimes heated debates relating to the introduction of new degree programs; the number, subject matter

3. I am indebted to historian Margaret Lamberts Bendroth for her description of Andover's early faculty, student body and curriculum. The specific quotations and descriptions in my account are taken from *A School of the Church*, 1–24. See especially pages 19–21. See also Timothy Dwight, *Sermon Preached at the Opening of the Theological Institution in Andover; and at the Ordination of Rev. Eliphalet Pearson, L.L.D. September 28, 1808* (Boston: Farrand, Mallory, and Co., 1808).

4. See for example *Gordon-Conwell Theological Seminary: 1970–1971* (Wenham, MA: Published by the Seminary, 1970), 23–24.

and significance of core requirements; and the naming, listing, and cross-listing of both old and new courses. Considerable attention was given, for example, to the pros and cons of adding a requirement in evangelism in the Master of Divinity degree program— with Christy Wilson making an impassioned and successful case for the change. On another occasion, during the 1978/1979 academic year, the faculty debated whether or not the seminary should add the Doctor of Ministry to its degree offerings. Feelings ran deep within the faculty with some strongly favoring the addition and others lining up in strong opposition. "Only over my dead body," remarked one faculty member, when asked if such a program would be approved. Gradually however, after many months of faculty discussion and debate, the resistance gave way and a new Doctor of Ministry degree—much stronger as a result of those debates—was approved by vote of the faculty and trustees by an overwhelming margin.[5] Curricular changes have certainly come, as these instances illustrate, but at Gordon-Conwell they have tended to be incremental.

5. Gordon-Conwell Theological Seminary, "Regular Faculty Meeting Minutes," from June 1970 through September 1992, two large notebooks housed at the seminary library. See also four file folders of "Curriculum Committee" minutes and materials and six files of "Dean's Council Minutes" (relating to curricular matters during the 1970s) in Harold John Ockenga Papers (Box 28) housed at Gordon-Conwell Theological Seminary. In the autumn of 1978, President Ockenga asked his newly-appointed Academic Dean, Garth Rosell, to work with the faculty in securing approval for a Doctor of Ministry degree program at the seminary. Joining hands with Carl Saylor, discussions were held throughout the 1978–79 academic year and by the May meeting of the faculty, a new Doctor of Ministry degree had been approved by a vote of twenty-four to three. The recommendation was then sent to the Board of Trustees for its review and eventual approval. Currently overseen by Dr. David Currie, a gifted administrator, it has proven to be one of the seminary's most resilient and successful programs.

Professor Christy Wilson

Such curricular stability in the preparation of pastors has, of course, been characteristic since the founding of the Christian church in the first century. While the three-year, Andover model seminary is a relatively recent development, the earlier patterns of training—be they university-based, monastic, or apprenticeship models—tended to have focused on basically the same curricular core: namely, a thorough understanding of the Bible accompanied by studies of Christian history, theology, ethics, preaching, philosophy, and the pastoral arts.[6] While President Woodrow Wilson may have been correct in his observation that "it is easier to move a cemetery than to change a curriculum," some members of the seminary's faculty have been prepared to argue that such continuity should be commended rather than condemned. After all, for

6. George M. Marsden and Bradley J. Longfield, eds., *The Secularization of the Academy* (New York: Oxford University Press, 1992); George M. Marsden, *The Soul of the American University* (New York: Oxford University Press, 1994); and Garth M. Rosell, "Engaging Issues in Course Development," in Malcolm L. Warfield, ed., *Practical Wisdom on Theological Teaching and Learning* (New York: Peter Lang, 2004), 181–96.

more than two thousand years certain core requirements have been considered essential, indeed non-negotiable, if those who have been called to "the art of arts" are to be adequately prepared.[7]

Professors Mott, Wilson, Peace, and Borgman

What complicates the discussion, of course, is what John Fletcher identified in 1980 as "the coming crisis in theological seminaries."[8] As late as the 1950s, Fletcher observed, most seminaries still had a single educational goal—namely, to train pastors for the church. By 1980, when Fletcher reported the findings of his study, virtually every theological institution in the Association of Theological Schools had already expanded its programs to offer continuing education for clergy, theological education for laity and ethical and theological reflection for churches, community leaders and the professions. "Seminaries are slowly but surely walking into a minefield," he predicted only a decade after the founding

7. J. I. Packer and Gary A. Parrett, *Grounded in the Gospel: Building Believers the Old-Fashioned Way* (Grand Rapids: Baker Books, 2010).

8. John Fletcher, "Beyond Survival: The Coming Crisis for Theological Seminaries," *Alban Institute Action Information* (November/December 1980), 6–10. See also *The Futures of Protestant Seminaries* (Washington, DC: The Alban Institute, 1983).

of Gordon-Conwell, if one takes seriously the significant changes that are occurring in student demographics, church membership, faculty aging patterns, growing economic pressures, and the trend toward professionalization. "In an era of increasingly fragmented seminary life and part-time attendance," Fletcher suggested, "opportunities for serious self-knowledge and mutual reflection on the student's ethical, educational and emotional background will be markedly fewer."[9]

Professors Kalland, Davis, Wells, and Nicole

Sensitive to these changing patterns, seminaries like Gordon-Conwell began to add new educational programs to their rosters, to increase the number and focus of their degree offerings and to radically expand the number of administrators needed to support, oversee and keep up with the growing demand.[10] Having largely resisted such changes for a decade and a half, a new culture of

9. Fletcher, "Beyond Survival," 6–10.

10. "We need continuing education!" wrote Dean Stuart Barton Babbage in an April 23, 1971 letter to pastors. Indeed, the seminary's minutes throughout the 1970s reflect dozens of discussions and actions relating to continuing education for clergy and laypersons in church, community and the professions.

growth and diversification began to emerge during the last half of the 1980s, 1990s, and into the 2000s. "Our vision is to do everything in our power under God to end our day's famine of God's Word," remarked President Walter Kaiser in 2005. "To this end we will train—more than ever before—evangelists, missionaries, pastors, and leaders for the cause of Christ. This is what motivates us as we move forward into an ambitious time of growth and strength.[11]

The seminary's catalog for 1980/1981 for example, shortly after the Fletcher study was released in 1980, described Gordon-Conwell's Master of Divinity degree program with the following words: The seminary's Master of Divinity program is "designed primarily for those who expect to enter the formal ministry: either the pastorate or in organizations associated with the work of the local church. It is, however, a flexible program and allows for special emphasis in the areas of evangelism, missions, urban studies, counseling, Christian education and allied interests."[12] Special tracks were provided in Urban Studies, Church Educational Ministry and Young Life Youth Ministries. In addition to the Master of Divinity, only two additional degrees were available in 1980: the Master of Religious Education and the Master of Theological Studies.

By 1985, the basic requirements for and description of the Master of Divinity degree had remained unchanged with one exception: namely, that the old Field Education program (with its four units of non-credit engagement) had been replaced by a new Supervised Ministry program with its two-course requirement. This

---

11. Walter C. Kaiser, Jr., in Gordon-Conwell Theological Seminary, *Self-Study Report 2005 for the Reaffirmation of Accreditation of Gordon-Conwell Theological Seminary*, prepared for the Association of Theological Schools and the New England Association of Schools and Colleges, Inc. (July 7, 2005), 19.

12. Gordon-Conwell Theological Seminary, *Catalog for 1980/1981*, 59. Thirty courses were needed to complete the degree including the following requirements: Old Testament (3 courses), New Testament (3), Theology (3), Church History (2), Greek (2), Hebrew (2), Christian Communications (2), Social Ethics (1), Christian Education (1), Ministry of the Church (1), World Missions (1), Pastoral Counseling (1), Field Education (4 units).

had resulted in the course requirements for the Master of Divinity degree being raised from thirty to thirty-two. Specialty "tracks" had been replaced by "concentrations" in Church Educational

Professors Goddard, Nicole, Michaels, Smick, and Kline

Ministry, Urban Studies, World Missions, and Youth Ministries. In addition to the Master of Divinity, the seminary offered the Master of Theological Studies, the Doctor of Ministry and the Master of Religious Education—with a new M.R.E. degree program added for the Center for Urban Ministerial Education (CUME) in Boston.[13]

By 1990, the requirements and description for the Master of Divinity degree program remained the same with the exception that two requirements in Supervised Ministry were decreased to one and the single requirement in the Ministry of the Church was increased to two. "Concentrations" were replaced by "tracks" in Church Educational Ministries, Urban Year, World Missions and Youth Ministries. New two year (20 course requirement) Master of

13. Gordon-Conwell Theological Seminary, *Catalog for 1985/1986*, 43–54.

Arts degree tracks were added in Christian Education, Counseling, Family Ministries, World Missions and Evangelism, Youth Ministries, and Religion. At CUME, in Boston, a new Master of Arts in Christian Education replaced the old M.R.E. degree program and a full Master of Divinity degree program in Urban Ministries was added.[14]

President Gerald Ford Speaking at his Son's Commencement

By 1995, the requirements and description for the Master of Divinity degree program remained the same but the Doctor of Ministry degree had begun using the language of a "Generalist Track" as distinguished from a "Specialist Mentoring Track." More striking was the seminary's addition of Master of Arts degree

14. Gordon-Conwell Theological Seminary, *Catalog for 1990/1991*, 41–59.

programs in Old Testament, New Testament, Church History, and Theology. These two-year, twenty-course degrees were designed for missionaries, teachers in public and Christian schools, and "for students who are intending to pursue university doctoral degrees after the completion of the M.A." The Master of Arts degrees in Christian Education, Counseling, World Missions and Evangelism and Religion along with the Doctor of Ministry degree and the old Master of Theology degree were all continued.[15]

Of even greater significance, were the establishment in 1992 of a new branch campus in Charlotte, North Carolina, and the establishment in 2004 of a new branch campus in Jacksonville, Florida. While the main campus in Hamilton, the seminary's only truly residential center, remains the primary engine of institutional administration, national and international reputation, financial and staff resources, and faculty strength, the branch campuses established by President Robert E. Cooley and President Walter Kaiser respectively have had a profound impact on both the seminary's curriculum and its understanding and practice of is basic mission. Those important stories, however, will need to wait until they can be taken up more fully in the later chapters of our study.[16]

Meanwhile, on the Hamilton campus, the requirements and descriptions for the Master of Divinity degree program at the turn of the century had reduced the requirement in number of courses from thirty-two to thirty by replacing the two-credits for Mentored Ministry to a non-credit requirement of six semesters. Pastoral Counseling's two-course requirement was reduced to one—and that credit course, thanks to the strong advocacy of Christy Wilson and others, was set aside for the new evangelism requirement.[17] In 2005, the Master of Arts degrees underwent some further refinement. Five "Academic Master of Arts degrees were designed

15. Gordon-Conwell Theological Seminary, *Catalog for 1995/1996*, 57–69.

16. For a brief introduction to the Charlotte story, see Robert J. Mayer, "Gordon-Conwell—Charlotte and Theological Education: Its History in Light of Emerging Trends," in the *Africanus Journal*, Vol. 8, No. 1 (April 2016), 39–48.

17. Gordon-Conwell Theological Seminary, *Catalog for 2000/2001*, 25–42.

to meet the needs of students who desire to gain knowledge of a particular academic field, and who are not planning on entering pastoral ministry in the Church for which the M.Div. is the appropriate degree." Seven professional Master of Arts degrees, on the other hand, were "designed to meet the needs of students who desire to gain preparation for professional ministry in church and parachurch settings, but who are not planning to become pastors."

Professor Wilson Praying with Students

By the time of the seminary's accreditation review in 2015, along with the Master of Divinity degree program—still considered "Gordon-Conwell's flagship degree on all campuses"—the seminary was offering ten Master of Arts professional degree programs and nine Master of Arts academic degree programs, the Doctor of Philosophy degree (in cooperation with Boston University), the Master of Theology degree and the multiple tracks of a rapidly expanding Doctor of Ministry degree program. On the eve of the seminary's fiftieth anniversary, with the subsequent addition of two more degree programs by vote of the faculty and board in 2018, Gordon-Conwell Theological Seminary was offering a total of twenty-five degree programs on four different campus settings. What had started in 1969 as a curriculum with three degree programs, two campus settings, a handful of administrators, one academic dean and a faculty of approximately twenty full-time members had grown by 2019 to a curriculum with twenty-five degree offerings, overseen by eight deans, sixteen senior administrators and a variety of program directors, offered on four different campuses and taught by a full-time faculty that had essentially only doubled in size.[18]

Like other tuition-dependent seminaries in the Association of Theological Schools, Gordon-Conwell seemed inclined to adopt a strategy of diversification and growth to prepare itself for the "coming crisis in theological seminaries" that John Fletcher had predicted in 1980. Well aware of the dramatic changes that were occurring in student demographics, church membership, the aging of faculty and the growth in educational costs, special attention was given to encourage student recruitment, student retention, expansion of the donor base, increasing the seminary's endowment and operating with greater efficiency. Undergirding those strategies was the creation of a culture of growth. New degrees and programs were added to attract potential students.

Professors Walters, Fillinger, Ensworth, and Pendleton

18. For the current statistics on faculty and administration see the seminary's website

Fresh attention was given to fund raising and enlarging the seminary's endowment. New partnerships were forged between the seminary and the church. Increased attention was given to new educational technologies and innovative delivery systems. The results, at least for a time, were encouraging. For most of the seminary's history, as we have seen, student enrollment continued to grow—establishing Gordon-Conwell Theological Seminary as one of the largest and most influential seminaries within the Association of Theological Schools. Such momentum, however, is almost impossible to maintain over time and for Gordon-Conwell the growth in enrollment—along with the tuition revenues that it produced—eventually began to level off and decline.

Professors Nicole, Kalland, Wilson, Rosell, Kerr, Wells, and Lovelace

Despite these and other challenges, however, there is reason to believe that the seminary's best days are yet ahead. While a culture of growth may no longer be a viable strategy for solving the seminary's financial challenges, a culture of excellence is certainly within reach. The seminary's founders, as the reader will recall, sought to create a seminary of about seven hundred students that could deserve to be called "one of the outstanding divinity schools in the world." They insisted on planting its main campus near Boston, the "Athens of America" as they liked to call it, so that the seminary would combine both actually and symbolically the very best of evangelical thinking and scholarship, the deepest devotion to Christ and his Word, the most urgent commitment to spreading the gospel to every woman, man, boy, and girl on the planet, the most thorough understanding of history, theology, and culture, the most winsome love for the church and for those it seeks to serve, and the most unflinching Christian discipleship, whatever the cost. While they could not have foreseen the expansion of the seminary into Charlotte and Jacksonville, they did hope, by God's grace, that the seminary—as long as God was pleased for it to exist—would represent the very best of what the old Puritans would have called "piety and learning."

The primary link to Boston's academic community was a consortium of theological schools known as the Boston Theological Institute. As early as 1972, in fact, Dean Stuart Barton Babbage recommended to the Board of Trustees, despite the surprisingly high cost of joining, that the seminary as soon as possible "apply for full membership in the Boston Theological Institute."[19] The benefits, Babbage argued, far outweighed any costs: since membership would allow Gordon-Conwell faculty and students access to libraries such as those at Harvard, Boston College, and Boston University; it would allow our students the privilege of taking credit courses at the other schools and allow their students to take courses on our campus; it would facilitate cooperation on "certain field work programs"; and it would provide "the opportunity" for faculty members to "share in professional gatherings" with the faculties of the other Boston schools. This relationship, Babbage argued, promises "to be a mutually beneficial one" and it "seems clear that Gordon-Conwell's role in the BTI will be an increasingly

19. Stuart Barton Babbage, "Dean's Report to the Board of Trustees," February 23 and October 21, 1972. The annual membership fees in the early 1970s was $12,500. Quotation taken from the February 23rd report, page 1. Copy in the Harold John Ockenga Papers housed at Gordon-Conwell Theological Seminary.

significant one. At a recent colloquium on 'Salvation Today,' the largest contingent of faculty and student representatives was from Gordon-Conwell." Then, concluding his remarks to the trustees, Babbage commented that "the next colloquium will be held on our campus."[20]

Boston Theological Institute Board of Trustees[21]

The administration was not alone, of course, in recognizing the importance of the seminary's connection with the BTI.[22] Da-

20. Stuart Barton Babbage, "Report of the Academic Dean to the Board of Trustees," October 21, 1972. Copy in the Harold John Ockenga Papers housed at Gordon-Conwell Theological Seminary.

21. Boston Theological Institute Board of Trustees in 1987. Front row (left to right): Dick Nesmith (Boston University), Edward M. O'Flaherty (Weston), George Peck (Andover Newton), Robert J. Daly (Boston College). Second row: A. C. Calivas (Holy Cross), Diana Small (BTI Staff), Garth Rosell (Gordon-Conwell), Lorine M. Getz (BTI Director), Thomas J. Daly (St. Johns), and Otis Charles (Episcopal Divinity School).

22. Brian Boisen, "A Brief History of the First Twenty-Five Years of the Boston Theological Institution," Master of Arts Thesis presented to the

vid Scholer, Professor of New Testament at the seminary, wrote Babbage in December of 1972 to thank him "in particular for his support of GCTS' membership in BTI."[23] Roger Nicole likewise, as Professor of Theology, wrote to thank the dean for his "leadership in the matter of our relationship to BTI."[24] The reason for their enthusiastic support and the willingness by the administration and board to provide the necessary funds to make it possible was the widely shared conviction that the seminary's engagement with Boston's academic community would help it to fulfill the founders' vision. Across its history, Gordon-Conwell Theological Seminary has aspired to attract the best and the brightest in both its faculty and its student body—not for the sake of some elitist ambition but from a desire to fulfill the greatest of all commandments: namely, that we are commanded as God's faithful followers to love the Lord our God with all our heart, all our soul, all our strength *and all our mind*. And, of course, as disciples of the Lord Jesus Christ we are commanded likewise to love our neighbor as ourselves.[25]

Department of Church History, Gordon-Conwell Theological Seminary, 1994. Garth M. Rosell (GCTS), Rodney Petersen (BTI Director), and Robert Daly (Boston College) served as Supervisory Readers.

23. Scholer to Babbage, December 4, 1972. Copy of letter in the Harold John Ockenga Papers (Box 28) housed at Gordon-Conwell Theological Seminary.

24. Nicole to Babbage, December 8, 1972. Copy of letter in the Harold John Ockenga Papers (Box 28) housed at Gordon-Conwell Theological Seminary.

25. Luke 10:27 (ESV)

CHAPTER VI

Establishing a Campus in Boston

Boston is the thinking center of the continent
and therefore of the planet[1]

—OLIVER WENDELL HOLMES

LONG BEFORE GORDON-CONWELL THEOLOGICAL Seminary had
ever become an institutional reality, its founders had already envisioned the special role within urban America they hoped, by God's
grace, that it would play. Both Russell Conwell and Adoniram
Judson Gordon, as we have seen, were pastors of congregations
located respectively in the heart of Philadelphia and Boston; both
knew first hand the important role that education could play in
addressing the growing needs of those who lived and worked in
the city; and both had established educational institutions to help
address those needs.[2]

With the merger of those two older institutions, the founders
of Gordon-Conwell Theological Seminary reaffirmed their interest in maintaining a significant presence in the city. With their

1. Quotation by Oliver Wendell Holmes taken from Kari Haskell, "Quotes
About Boston," *New York Times* (July 23, 2004).

2. See chapter I, "The History Before the History"

missional goals of having both a "suburban campus" and an "urban campus," they envisioned that the first would be established near Boston and the second in the heart of Philadelphia.[3] Although they were unsuccessful in their efforts to establish the campus in Philadelphia, both Babbage and Ockenga hoped that such a campus could soon be established in the center of Boston. Those dreams finally became a reality in the autumn of 1976, when the Center for Urban Ministerial Education officially opened its doors in Roxbury, Massachusetts for the very first time. "We started with 30 students," recalls Eldin Villafane, its founding director, at the Second African Meeting House on 11 Moreland Street."[4]

CUME's Founding Director, Eldin Villafane

3. Harold John Ockenga, "Reflections on a Decade of Service," an interview with Bob Hoock published in *The Paper* (9 April 1979), 1. "Billy [Graham], Mr. [J. Howard] Pew and I sat down [at the time of the merger] and we outlined what we thought were going to be the goals for Gordon-Conwell."

4. Steve Daman, "The City Gives Birth to a Seminary," in the *Africanus Journal* (April 2016), Vol. 8, No. 1, 33–38. Quotation is taken from page 35.

"About 16 were Latinos and 12 were African Americans, and maybe one or two were White." Few could possibly have imagined as the thirty students gathered for the first time that those relatively modest beginnings would eventually produce what is now widely considered to be one of the premier urban theological training programs in the world today—having become a model for contextual urban theological education that continues to be studied and copied in cities around the globe.

As with many young institutions, however, the actual story of how the seminary moved from the founders' visionary goals in 1969 to an actual classroom filled with thirty students in 1976 is complex, largely undocumented and frequently shrouded in mystery. When asked how it all began, in fact, one of its early leaders responded—with a mischievous twinkle in his eye—"Which version would you like to hear?" After all, as president John F. Kennedy liked to remark, "success has many fathers but failure is an orphan."

What is clear, in the providence of God, is that more than twenty uniquely gifted individuals—and perhaps others unknown or unheralded—made absolutely essential contributions to the development of the Center for Urban Theological Education during its early years. Among these were Harold John Ockenga, Lloyd Kalland, Michael Haynes, Ricardo Tanon, Eldin and Margie Villafane, VaCountess Johnson, Stephen Mott, Dean Borgman, Doug and July Hall, W. Nigel Kerr, Sam Hogan, Soliny Vedrine, Ruy Costa, Bruce Wall, Gene Neville, Rudy Mitchell, Web Brower, Naomi Wilshire, Efrain Agosto, Ira Frazier, and Lorraine Anderson. While each of these remarkable individuals is deserving of special attention, it seemed to have been the blending of their individual contributions into a cohesive and interconnected whole that God was pleased to use in making CUME a reality. Visionary pastors like Michael Haynes, Ricardo Tanon, Soliny Vedrine, Bruce Wall, and Ruy Costa; bookstore managers like Web Brower; supportive administrators like Harold John Ockenga, Lloyd Kalland and Nigel Kerr; committed faculty members like Steve Mott, Bob Pazmino and Dean Borgman; researchers like Rudy Mitchell; and gifted urban ministry specialists like Doug and Judy Hall, Eldin and Margie Villafane, Sam Hogan, VaCountess Johnson, Naomi Wilshire, Ira Frazier, Lorraine Anderson, and Efrain Agosto all joined hands in common cause. What had seemed almost impossible at the start of the 1970s was by 1976 a vital, functioning reality—destined, by God's grace, not only to change the religious landscape in Boston and throughout New England but also, by its example, the shape of urban theological education around the globe.

What held it all together during those early years, of course, were the savvy leadership, pastoral skills, and tireless labors of Eldin and Margie Villafane. Having served for several years as the Director of Christian Education for the largest Hispanic Assemblies of God congregation in America—the *Iglesia Christiana Juan 3:16* church in New York City—Eldin and Margie took up their student lodgings at Boston University in 1973. Having been urged to continue his education by Ricardo Tanon, the senior pastor of *John 3:16*, Eldin had come to Boston to pursue the Ph.D. degree in social ethics. Eldin and Margie planned to return to New York City upon completion of his degree to continue their work at *John 3:16*.[5]

Not long after arriving in Boston, however, Eldin found himself in a little bookstore on Shawmut Avenue that was "bursting with books and music in both Spanish and English," as Steve Daman has so beautifully described the scene, "furnished with vintage display counters and decorated with brightly painted maracas, guiros, tambourines, and a variety of flags. The little store seemed dark at first coming off the street," Eldin reported, "yet the room was always full of cheerful conversation, lively music, and warm Christian fellowship. Eldin struck up a friendship with the manager, Web Brower, who had launched the store in 1970 as a ministry of the Emmanuel Gospel Center (EGC). The store served as a resource center for the growing Hispanic church community

---

5. Biographical materials are taken largely from the author's oral history interview with Eldin Villafane, February 21, 2012, in the GMR Papers housed at the seminary.

as thousands of Latinos were moving into Boston from across Latin America as well as from New York and Puerto Rico."[6]

Emmanuel Gospel Center Bookstore

Upon discovering Eldin's previous experience as a Director of Christian Education in New York City, Web invited him to help plan a Christian Education Conference that was being designed for Boston. "They asked me to mobilize some Latinos," as Eldin described the process in our interview, "hoping that I might be able to round-up twenty or thirty Spanish-speaking believers who might be interested in such a conference.[7] Well," to their great surprise, "I was able to recruit over three hundred!" The leaders of the conference, including Michael Haynes, Bruce Wall, and VaCountess Johnson from Twelfth Baptist Church, were not only impressed by his obvious organizational skills but by the reputation that he

6. Steve Daman, "The City Gives Birth to a Seminary," in the *Africanus Journal*, Vol. 8, No. 1 (April 2016), 33. Daman provides the reader with a delightfully insightful introduction to the early years of CUME. See also the Gordon-Conwell *Contact: Graduation 1979*, Vol. 9, No. 4 (Summer 1979), 16.

7. Oral History Interview, Eldin Villafane and Garth Rosell, December 5, 2012, GMR Papers, Gordon-Conwell Theological Seminary.

enjoyed within the broader Christian church. The conference also deepened his involvement with the Emmanuel Gospel Center and its founders, Doug and Judy Hall, and earned him a series of invitations to speak at some of its events.

Consequently, when Gordon-Conwell launched its own urban program in 1973—under the leadership of Steve Mott, Dean Borgman, Nigel Kerr, Doug Hall, and a handful of others and known within the seminary as the Urban Middler Year program— it seemed almost inevitable that Eldin would become part of the program.[8] So it came as no surprise when during the summer of 1976 he was appointed to serve as Assistant Professor of Christianity and Society and Director of the Center for Urban Ministerial Education.[9]

Located in the Martin Luther King House adjacent to Twelfth Baptist Church, the new center was designed to provide "education for ministers and church leaders who have not had the advantage of full formal education" and to provide classes for "those who desire to study beyond their seminary training."[10] The needs of the city are important, remarked Dr. Michael Haynes, pastor of Twelfth Baptist Church, longtime trustee of the seminary, and among the strongest advocates for the establishment of CUME,

8. Students enrolled in the program were expected to live in the city during their second full year of study, to serve in an inner-city church and to take classes at the Emmanuel Gospel Center. For a description of the program see "Gordon-Conwell Goes to Boston," *Contact* magazine, Vol. 4, No. 2 (Graduation Issue 1973), 4–5. See also "Seminarians Involved with Needs of Youth in Greater Boston Area," *Contact*, Vol. 4, No. 3 (Spring 1974), 4–6; "Blacks' Conference and City Workshop Involve Seminary People," *Contact*, Vol. 6, No. 3 (Spring 1976), 3; "The Center Celebrates," *Contact*, Vol. 9, No. 4 (Summer 1979), 16; "Ministry in the City," special issue of *Contact* magazine, Vol. 16, No. 1 (1987); and "Seeking the Peace of the City: Ministry in the Urban Context," special issue of *Contact* magazine, Vol. 35, No. 1 (Summer 2005).

9. "Urban Center is Launched; Villafane Becomes Director," *Contact*, Vol. 7, No. 1 (Fall 1976), 1–2. The name of the new center, the Center for Urban Ministerial Education (CUME), was first suggested by VaCountess Johnson, Assistant Director of the program. Eldin Villafane was succeeded as Director of CUME by four gifted leaders: Efrain Agosto, Alvin Padilla, Mark G. Harden and Seong Hyun Park.

10. *Contact*, Vol. 7, No. 1 (Fall 1976), 1–2.

and there will surely "be rejoicing in the souls of those who benefit from the skills and training received in this program." With about thirty students, an eight-course curriculum and instructors from both the seminary and the city, the new center opened for business in the fall of 1976.[11] Within three years, its course offerings and student population had more than doubled.[12] Within five years, as hundreds of people gathered for the center's fifth graduation celebration at Twelfth Baptist Church, they learned that CUME had not only granted a total of 738 certificates and twenty diplomas by the seminary's graduation in 1981 but that a much anticipated accredited master's degree program had also been approved.[13] Indeed, by the time that the 1982 graduation arrived, CUME's very first MRE graduates were awarded their degrees along with a leather-bound Bible presented by Professor Eldin Villafane![14]

11. Those teaching the courses were Steve Mott, Dean Borgman, Bob Fill-inger, Eldin Villafane, VaCountess Johnson, Eugene Neville, Samuel Hogan and Louis Robles.

12. "The Center Celebrates," *Contact*, Vol. 9, No. 4 (Summer Issue 1979), 16.

13. *Contact*, Vol. 11, No. 3 (Graduation 1981), 15. "One of the special events of the evening," the article reported, "was the presentation by Gordon-Conwell Academic Dean Garth Rosell outlining the new Master of Religious Education degree program to be offered by CUME beginning in the 1981–82 academic year."

14. The recipients were the Rev. Thomas Watson, the Rev. Estaban Soto, the Rev. Natividad Rivera, the Rev. Phillip Galloway, the Rev. Marie Gaston, the Rev. Fernando Del Orbe, the Rev. Theodore N. Hester, Sr. and the Rev. Glenfield Prescod (*in absentia*). *Contact*, Vol. 12, No. 2 (Commencement Issue 1982), 4.

The Rev. Dr. Michael Haynes

Along with Eldin and Margie Villafane, two who certainly played the primary role in the establishment of CUME, two other individuals deserve special mention: namely Michael Haynes and Harold John Ockenga. Without their encouragement, support, and unswerving commitment, CUME would never have become a reality.

"The tragic assassination of my personal friend and former colleague Martin Luther King, Jr. in April of 1968," remarked the Rev. Dr. Michael Haynes in May of 2000 at CUME's twenty-fifth anniversary celebration in Cambridge, led to a violent eruption of the "long-brewing racial volcano" in America's urban centers.[15] "Before the Atlanta funeral of Dr. King," Haynes continued, "an ecumenical memorial service was held at the Parkman Bandstand on the Boston Common. As a long time personal friend of Martin

15. Dr. Michael Haynes delivered this deeply moving speech at a gala celebration held in honor of CUME's 25th anniversary at the Royal Sonesta Hotel in Cambridge, Massachusetts in May of 2000. Virginia G. Viola transcribed the address and it has been included in this account with only minor changes.

and Coretta, a member of the [Massachusetts] House of Representatives, and pastor of an historic, King-related church, I was
invited to be one of the speakers. Sitting on the stage, in the row
behind me, as a non-participating distinguished guest, was the late
Dr. Harold John Ockenga. I had known him most of my life from a
distance. He was a positive influence in my life. He was just getting
to know me."

"Four years earlier, during my first campaign for election to
the Mass. House of Representatives," Dr. Haynes continued,

> two members of Dr. Ockenga's congregation had come
> into my life as supporters, encouragers, and prayer inter-
> cessors. They were Alan Emery, Jr., a key Park Street lay
> leader and prominent businessman, and Roger Dewey, a
> young social activist and leader among the Park Street's
> university students. These two laypersons became sig-
> nificant links to the inner city community. Both of them
> were becoming channels that would help unite discon-
> nected groupings of the body of Christ. Another vital
> link at work during the pre-King assassination years
> was a humble, quiet, sincere minister, Doug Hall of Em-
> manuel Gospel Center in the South End. In a sense, each
> of these persons would become "Midwives" at the birth
> of this significant theological training ministry we now
> know as CUME.

Professor Richard Peace Congratulates CUME MRE Graduate Kelly McLean

"Something was already stirring in the heart of Dr. Ockenga as he sat at the Parkman Bandstand that day," continued Dr. Haynes.

> Never before had I ever witnessed Dr. Ockenga in attendance at an affair which brought together all of the secular and religious leaders of the Black Community. But here we were—Black and White, Catholic, Protestant, Jew, Muslim and Agnostic. The Holy Spirit was preparing Harold John for a new adventure: the birth of this vital ministry. At the close of that memorial service, Dr. Ockenga approached me saying, "I would like to sit down and chat with you soon." God was setting in motion a new thing for a new day. A number of formal and informal meetings took place in the days and years ahead between white and concerned evangelicals and a small group of blacks and other inner city workers of evangelical persuasion.[16]

Dr. Haynes then concluded his remarks with the following words:

> Harold John Ockenga—who for over three decades had made the cosmos, the globe, his great commission concern—had at last heard the cry . . . to "come on home!" to come back home! Harold John Ockenga, one of the principal architects of the evangelical movement worldwide had finally come to Black Roxbury and in so doing he would come to Latino Boston and Haitian Boston and Cape Verdean Boston and in so doing he would become an active partner in producing a new generation of sensitive, well-equipped men and women, grounded in Biblical orthodoxy and a high view of Scripture to proclaim

---

16. On one such occasion, Dean Borgman—his old automobiles packed with seminary students excited about ministry in the city—picked-up Harold John Ockenga at his home in Hamilton, Massachusetts an drove him down to Boston for a Chinese meal with Haynes, Paul Toms, Eugene Neville, Doug Hall, and others. On the way back to Hamilton, as Professor Borgman describes the conversation, Dr. Ockenga not only committed himself to support the Boston program but solicited support for the venture on his regular radio broadcast.

and bring God's love in Christ Jesus as the hope for the inner city.

Indeed, remarked Dr. Haynes,

Harold John Ockenga had received a new vision of the inner city! God bless Dr. Ockenga's baby on its 25th birthday. God bless your memory, Harold John—and as St. Paul says to the Thessalonians, "We give thanks to God always for you, remembering without ceasing your work of faith and labor of love, and patience of hope in our Lord Jesus Christ, in the sight of God our Father." The Center for Urban Ministerial Education shines today as a foretaste pictured in the words of that old second-coming chorus: "When the roll is called up yonder; I'll be filled with joy and wonder; When I see that blood-bought number, Some of every tribe and nation will be there."[17]

Contextualized Urban Theological Education

What has helped to make the CUME project such a success was its commitment to contextualized urban theological education. "To 'contextualize' means you have to keep listening to the needs of the city," explains Villafane. "Three overarching objectives" comprise CUME's curricular foundation: namely, (1) the formation of the people of God (2) "by informing them about Scripture, tradition, reason and experience in social, cultural and concrete historical contexts, so that (3) they may serve as agents of transformation in their churches and communities." Indeed, he continued, the "curriculum involves not just the content to be communicated, but also the processes by which this occurs. Thus, what is 'taught' through example or ethos (the implicit curriculum), and what is not taught (the null curriculum), combines with the actual course offerings

---

17. A copy of Dr. Haynes' powerful address, from which the paragraphs above have been taken, can be found in the GMR Papers housed at Gordon-Conwell Theological Seminary.

and policies (the explicit or manifest curriculum) to create the total curricular vehicle in which the student participates."[18]

Bill Spencer Teaching a Class at CUME

From the beginning, Villafane notes, we offered "classes in English and Spanish." Soon we added courses in French and Creole for the growing Haitian community, Portuguese for growing Brazilian communities and even in American Sign Language for the hearing impaired. "As CUME got momentum, there was, at the same time, robust church planting in Boston, particularly among these migrant populations." God seemed pleased to use the churches, the Center for Urban Ministerial Education and the Emmanuel Gospel Center, Eldin believes, as "institutional 'feeders'" to both nurture and train the growing population touched by what has come to be called Boston's "Quiet Revival"—the remarkable movement of God's Spirit that has not only doubled the number of churches but has also tripled church attendance in the greater Boston area over the past fifty years. Today, as Steve Daman has noted, "Gordon-Conwell Theological Seminary—Boston (CUME) serves 300 students" each semester, "representing nearly forty denominations and twenty countries."[19]

18. Quotations from Eldin Villafane, "Contextualized Urban Theological Education: The Center for Urban Ministerial Education's Guiding Philosophy," *Contact* magazine, Vol. 35, No. 1 (Summer 2005), 27; and Steve Daman, "The City Gives Birth to a Seminary," in the *Africanus Journal*, Vol. 8, No. 1 (April 2016), 35–37.

19. Steve Damon, "The City Gives Birth to a Seminary" in the *Africanus Journal*, Vol. 8, No. 1 (April 2016), 35–37; and Doug Hall, "The Quiet Revival:

The CUME Campus in Roxbury, Massachusetts

As CUME has grown, however, its need for additional space has also grown. By God's grace, a beautiful new facility was provided to house the classes, provide library space, and to provide for needed administrative offices.[20] God has been pleased to bless and prosper these new facilities and use them to further enlarge the growing influence of the seminary's urban program.

"It is no accident," wrote Robert Wood Lynn, the longtime Vice-President for Religion at the Lilly Endowment, "that one of the liveliest centers for the education of people in urban ministry today" is "the nationally known work of the Center for Urban Ministerial Education."[21]

Nurturing the Vitality of the Church in the Context of the Broader Urban Community," *Contact*, Vol. 31, No. 1 (Summer 2001), 4–5, 14–17.

20. Alvin Padilla, "The Center for Urban Ministerial Education (CUME): An Historical Overview," *Contact* magazine, Vol. 35, No. 1 (Summer 2005), 30–31; and Eldin Villafane, Contextualized Urban Theological Education: The Center For Urban Ministerial Education's Guiding Philosophy," *Contact* magazine, Vol. 35, No. 1 (Summer 2005), 26–27.

21. Robert Wood Lynn, "The Evangelical Contribution to Theological Education," in Garth M. Rosell, ed., *The Vision Continues: Centennial Papers of Gordon-Conwell Theological Seminary* (So. Hamilton, MA: by the Seminary, 1992), 66–79.

CHAPTER VII

Adopting a Mission Statement

Without a mission statement, you may get to the top of the ladder
and then realize it was leaning against the wrong building.

—DAVE RAMSEY

A "GRAND STRATEGY," AS Yale's Pulitzer Prize winning historian
John Lewis Gaddis has suggested in his book *On Grand Strategy*,
is "the alignment of potentially unlimited aspirations with neces-
sarily limited capabilities. If you seek ends beyond your means," he
argued, "then sooner or later you'll have to scale back your ends to
fit your means. Expanding means may attain more ends, but not
all because ends can be infinite and means can never be. Whatever
balance you strike, there'll be a link between what's real and what's
imagined: between your current location and your intended desti-
nation. You won't have a strategy," Gaddis concluded, "until you've
connected these dots—dissimilar though they are—within the
situation in which you're operating."[1]

The growing aspirations of Gordon-Conwell Theological Seminary from one decade to the next, to apply the Gaddis

1. John Lewis Gaddis, *On Grand Strategy* (New York: Penguin Press, 2018),
21.

thesis to the seminary's experience, slowly began to outdistance its means and capabilities. The institution's expanding menu of offerings was beginning to place increasing pressure on its budget and personnel. Happily, with its size and academic reputation, Gordon-Conwell, throughout much of the twentieth century, was able to remain in a relatively strong position to weather the challenges. While some on campus would surely have echoed White Rabbit's lament in Lewis Carroll's classic, *Alice in Wonderland*— "the hurrier I go the behinder I get"—the seminary's increasing student population, savvy fund-raising programs, attractive student aid packages, strategic tightening of the fiscal belt, generosity of donors, expansion from two campuses to four, addition of new degree and educational programs, development of a strong distance education program and a variety of other creative initiatives helped to maintain the seminary's student enrollment and its reputation as a leader in North American theological education.

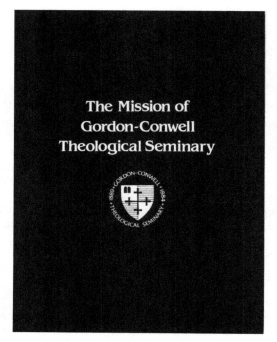

The Mission of
Gordon-Conwell
Theological Seminary

Among the primary reasons for the seminary's success in weathering the late twentieth-century storms were the clarity, community ownership, and operational role of Gordon-Conwell's Statement of Mission and the theological stability that was provided by the seminary's Basis of Faith.[2] The Statement of Mission, the younger of the two foundational documents, was especially useful in providing missional stability for the seminary in the midst of increasingly difficult challenges. In addition, it has proved to be a most valuable tool in the selection and evaluation of faculty, in the development of budgets, in the adoption of new courses and in the introduction of new degrees and new educational programs. Throughout the dozens of oral interviews conducted for this history, in fact, the seminary's Statement of Mission was not only frequently cited but it was warmly embraced, valued and appropriated by virtually everyone in the seminary community.[3]

Appointment of the Task Force

Among Robert E. Cooley's most important achievements during his years as president of the seminary was his decision, soon after arriving on campus, to establish a Task Force to prepare a comprehensive mission statement "in order to give direction to the future of the Seminary."[4] Equally important for the success of the project

2. *The Mission of Gordon-Conwell Theological Seminary* (So Hamilton, MA: by the seminary, 1983 [first printing], 1987 [second printing], 1990 [third printing]); and *The Mission of Gordon-Conwell Theological Seminary, Revised* (So. Hamilton, MA: by the seminary, 1992 [first printing], 1995 [second printing]). The total number of copies printed was 23,000). Adopted at the founding of the seminary, the seven articles of the Basis of Faith, discussed later in the chapter, have been reproduced annually in many of the institution's publications.

3. Recorded oral history interviews can be found in the GMR Papers housed at the seminary.

4. *The Mission of Gordon-Conwell Theological Seminary* (So. Hamilton, MA: by the Seminary, 1983), 2. Among the mandates given to President Cooley by the Board of Trustees (as he began his presidency) was the need, using the words of his predecessor, to "put the seminary in order." Although it was still a relatively young, collegial and visionary institution, Gordon-Conwell's

was his decision to appoint the seminary's respected theologian, David Wells, to chair the fifteen-member committee.[5] Appointed on October 23, 1981, the Task Force—representing faculty, administration, staff, students, alumni, and community—invested more than a year in meetings, consultations, document drafts, reviews, and rewrites before it was ready to present its findings to President Cooley for his review. Their final draft was presented to the president in December of 1982 and was subsequently passed along to the Seminary Goals Committee of the Board of Trustees for its review and recommendation. Completing its own study during the spring of 1983, the Seminary Goals Committee then presented the Statement of Mission to the full Board of Trustees for their consideration. On May 26, 1983, at its regular spring meeting, the full Board of Trustees voted unanimously to adopt the document as the seminary's official statement of mission.[6]

---

rapid growth had brought it to a point of complexity that required the development of formal structures (bylaws, handbooks, policy manuals, mission statements, organizational charts, etc.) and a new governance model (moving the seminary from the more informal "collegial governance" to carefully designed "shared governance") to make continued growth and sustainability possible. During the early years of his presidency, much of his time and energy was devoted to those tasks.

5. The fifteen members of the committee, chaired by David Wells, represented the faculty (Royce Gruenler, William Nigel Kerr, Douglas Stuart, Robert Fillinger, Gwyn Walters, Christy Wilson and David Wells), the administration and staff (Louise Cary, Robert Dvorak, Shirley Kerr, Wesley Roberts and Carlyle Saylor), the student body (John Hanford and Edward Keazirian), the alumni;/alumnae (Richard Schoenert) and the Hamilton community (Richard Thurber). Although its size made it somewhat unwieldy, it was President Cooley's desire to make sure it represented the entire seminary community.

6. Robert E. Cooley, "The Inside View," *Contact Magazine*, Winter 1984 (Volume 13, Number 4), 2.

David F. Wells, Task Force Chair

Ten thousand copies of the twenty-four-page document, printed with a distinctive dark blue cover during August of 1983, were widely distributed both on campus and beyond. "I am confident that the future depends upon the distinctive intellectual and spiritual vision to which the trustees, faculty and administration stand committed," wrote President Cooley in his introduction to the document, "and upon the overriding determination to bring that vision to the highest point of realization with the help of our God."[7]

Preamble

The seminary's Statement of Mission consists of three integral and interrelated sections: a one-page "preamble," a one-page listing of its six major articles and a twenty-page "commentary." In its relatively brief "preamble," readers are immediately reminded of the fact that "Gordon-Conwell Theological Seminary is first and foremost an "educational institution" with the primary mission of teaching, encouraging learning, and preparing "men and women for ministry at home and abroad." While such an affirmation might have seemed self-evident in earlier years, there are in our own day far too many who have come to see seminaries as more akin to therapeutic centers, spiritual retreat locations or even church substitutes rather than rigorous, demanding educational institutions. Seminaries are neither churches nor are they intended to be churches—although they are most certainly servants of Christ's church and partners with the church in its work—and they most assuredly are not intended to be mini-retreats, diploma mills, or comfortable places to spend a few years. Of all the fields for which educational training is required—from medical doctors to military officers—spiritual leadership should be the most rigorous and demanding. It is, as Gregory the Great phrased it many years ago, the "art of arts"—calling forth from each participant the deepest

---

7. Robert E. Cooley, "Introduction," *The Mission of Gordon-Conwell Theological Seminary* (South Hamilton, MA: by the seminary, 1983), 2. Early in 1991, wrote President Cooley in 1992, "ten years after the original task force began to meet, a smaller committee was established to review this Mission Statement, but only in the degree of its clarity at a few minor points. The committee completed its work confident that this Mission Statement, which has served the Seminary so well in the past, will continue to do so in the future as the institution prepares itself to move into the next millennium." The revised Statement of Mission was unanimously approved by the Board of Trustees on January 24, 1992 and was published (in a distinctive red cover) in August of 1992.

dedication, the most demanding discipline and the most ardent devotion. Members of the seminary community are, after all, servants of the living God.

Like the opening movements of a great symphony, the preamble also introduced important themes that were explored more fully throughout the articles and commentary. The seminary, for example, is declared to be "a training partner with the Church so that what is learned on campus may be complemented by the spiritual nurture and the exercise of ministry available through the Church." The foundational principles on which it operates, moreover, are "the centrality of Christ's saving work and the abiding truth of God's written Word." Its "institutional identity," furthermore, is "a result of its past history and the understanding of its present mission"—guarding "the essentials of the Reformation faith" while allowing "freedom in the formulation of non-essentials." It is "firmly evangelical" while maintaining "professional relations with schools of different theological persuasions." It is "committed both to academic excellence and practical relevance, both to personal piety and social responsibility, both to historic orthodoxy and its expression in language and actions understandable in the modern world." It is "interdenominational" while "warmly supportive of the denominations." It is "committed to the Church while also opening its programs to those who will not be preparing for service in traditional congregational settings." It is committed to "ministry in New England" but its "vision is also national and international."

Professor Ed Keazirian, Director of the Greek Language Program

Six Articles

At the heart of the Statement of Mission are its six articles—each of which

> arises out of God's redemptive work in this world effected in Jesus Christ, understood through the biblical Word, and mediated by the Holy Spirit. As a theological seminary, it provides learning, resources, and training through which men and women may acquire knowledge, gain skills, and develop attitudes needed in Christ's ministry. It's mission, accordingly, is to serve the Church in the following ways:

Article 1: To encourage students to become knowledgeable of God's inerrant Word, competent in its interpretation, proclamation and application in the contemporary world. Because the teaching of God's Word is indispensable to the well-being and vitality of God's people, the Seminary has a fundamental responsibility to encourage in students a love for Scripture. It is to teach exegetical skills by which they will be enabled to interpret the Word and inculcate understanding by which they will be able to apply it effectively.

Article 2: To maintain academic excellence in the highest tradition of Christian scholarship in the teaching of the biblical, historical and theological disciplines. Theological education, which is properly done within and for the Church, ought to function with rigor and academic integrity. The Seminary, therefore, must provide an environment within which teaching and learning can best occur and encourage high levels of scholarly competence and research in its faculty.

Article 3: To train and encourage students, in cooperation with the Church, to become skilled in ministry. The Church and Seminary share the goal of seeing knowledge, skills and attitudes integrated in the person who ministers. Both in traditional degree programs and in continuing education a combination of careful training and supervised experience in ministry are educational practices essential to achieving that goal.

Article 4: To work with the Churches towards the maturing of students so that their experiential knowledge of God in Christ is evidenced in their character, outlook, conduct, relationships and involvement in society. Academic learning divorced from a life of biblical spirituality neither honors God nor serves his people. Such spirituality is to be expressed cognitively, relationally and socially. It is to be translated into action, God's people embodying his compassion, declaring his justice and articulating his truth in society.

Professors Aida Spencer (New Testament) and Karen Mason, Director of the Hamilton Counseling Department

Article 5: To provide leadership and educational resources for shaping an effective evangelical presence in Church and society. Gordon-Conwell's academic and institutional resources are to be put in the service of the Christian community to provide careful research on and informed understanding of critical issues, as well as in exercising leadership in learned societies, in movements of renewal and reform, and in a variety of off-campus ministries in order to develop a more informed understanding of what the lordship of Christ means in our contemporary world.

Article 6: To develop in students a vision for God's redemptive work throughout the world and to formulate strategies that will lead to effective missions, evangelism and discipleship. The central mission of the triune God is the creation of a fellowship of men and women who are mature in Christ and who will love and serve him forever. This mission is realized evangelistically through the proclamation of the biblical gospel by those who embody and message they proclaim and who seek to make disciples from among all peoples.

Julie and Timothy Tennent[8]

Commentary

To properly understand the six relatively brief articles, it is necessary to consult with regularity the much fuller discussion of each within the commentary. Indeed, it would be as fruitless to separate the preamble and articles from the commentary—to borrow a picturesque image from the writings of Leonard I. Sweet—as it would be to unscramble a scrambled egg. The admirable brevity of the articles can lead to misunderstanding and misinterpretations when either the preamble or the commentary is removed. Those

8. Professor Timothy C. Tennent joined the faculty in 1998 and served for over a decade as the anchor for Gordon-Conwell's outstanding missions program. In 2009, Tim and Julie moved to Wilmore, Kentucky where Tim assumed his new responsibilities as President of Asbury Theological Seminary.

who penned the words intended them to work together as integral components of a single whole.

Like the opening preamble, the commentary begins with an affirmation of the two principles that "represent what is non-negotiable at Gordon-Conwell"—the "twin convictions" of "the abiding truth of God's written Word and the centrality of Christ's saving work." These "principles"—the formal and the material as they are classically known—"constitute the center of the Seminary's theological commitment," the "*sine qua non* for a coherent and effective educational program." If the Seminary's understanding of these principles should ever weaken, the document's writers and subscribers were convinced, its "usefulness as a center of Christian learning would be vitiated and its relationship to the broader evangelical movement jeopardized."

These two principles form the context within which the use of such descriptive words as "evangelical," "pluralism," "unity and purity," "truth," "church," and "ministry" must be understood and applied. "Evangelicalism," for example, is not, therefore, being defined in this statement by ethnic or class interests, nor by political or ideological distinctives, but by theology. For this reason theological identity is paramount at Gordon-Conwell in the selection of faculty members and in the education of the students. It is thus that we earn our name of being Gordon-Conwell *Theological* Seminary." With these foundational commitments in mind, the commentary explores each of the six articles in more detail.

Basis of Faith

A second major reason that the seminary was able to weather so many late twentieth-century challenges was its unswerving commitment to the Basis of Faith.[9] This seven-article doctrinal affirmation, drawn largely from an earlier Gordon Divinity School

9. The Gordon-Conwell Basis of Faith, published annually in the seminary catalog. See for example *Gordon-Conwell Theological Seminary Catalog 1975/1976* (So. Hamilton, Massachusetts: published by the seminary, 1975), 16.

statement, contains "a high view of Scripture," gives "expression to
the cardinal doctrines of the Reformed faith," and undergirds the
six articles of the Statement of Mission. Indeed, it would hardly be
an overstatement to claim that the Basis of Faith and the Statement
of Mission, when taken together, have formed the bedrock foundation on which Gordon-Conwell Theological Seminary, through
God's grace and favor, has been able to emerge as such a significant
center in the training of women and men for Christian ministry.[10]
The two documents are inextricably interconnected as the writers
of the Statement of Mission were unambiguously aware.

"This Mission Statement, in exploring these themes and in
developing the commentary which follows, is not offering an alter-
native to the existing Basis of Faith," as expressed in the preamble
to the commentary. "The Basis of Faith is primary and the Mission Statement, with respect to matters of belief, is derivative and
explanatory. What this statement does is to take the items of belief
to which the Seminary assents and to derive from these both the
principles by which this educational institution should shape its
life and the goals which it should struggle to attain if it is to serve
the Church most effectively. It is thus an application," the preamble
asserts, "of the Basis of Faith, not a substitute for it or an addition
to it."[11]

---

10. *Gordon-Conwell Theological Seminary Catalog 1970/1971* (Wenham,
MA: published by the seminary, 1970), 10–11.

11. *The Mission of Gordon-Conwell Theological Seminary* (So. Hamilton,
MA: published by the seminary, 1992), 4.

Professors Scott Hafemann and Gary Pratico

Having already explored some of the ways in which the Statement of Mission has sought to apply the Basis of Faith, it would be well for us to present—as the reader will find immediately below—the one document that has guided the seminary from the earliest days of its founding, namely its Basis of Faith. "We believe," reads the document, "that . . .

> I. The sixty-six canonical books of the Bible as originally written were inspired of God, hence free from error. They constitute the only infallible guide in faith and practice.

> II. There is one God, the Creator and Preserver of all things, infinite in being and perfection. He exists eternally in three Persons; the Father, the Son and the Holy Spirit, who are of one substance and equal in power and glory.

> III. Man, created in the image of God, through disobedience fell from his sinless state at the suggestion of Satan. This fall plunged man into a state of sin and spiritual

death, and brought upon the entire race the sentence of eternal death. From this condition man can be saved only by the grace of God, through faith, on the basis of the work of Christ, and by the agency of the Holy Spirit.

IV. The eternally pre-existent Son became incarnate without human father, by being born of the virgin Mary. Thus in the Lord Jesus Christ divine and human natures were united in one Person, both natures being whole, perfect and distinct. To effect salvation, He lived a sinless life and died on the cross as the sinner's substitute, shedding His blood for the remission of sins. On the third day He rose from the dead in the body which had been laid in the tomb. He ascended to the right hand of the Father, where He performs the ministry of intercession. He shall come again, personally and visibly, to complete His saving work and to consummate the eternal plan of God.

V. The Holy Spirit is the third Person of the Triune God. He applies to man the work of Christ. By justification and adoption man is given a right standing before God; by regeneration, sanctification and glorification man's nature is renewed.

VI. The believer, having turned to God in penitent faith in the Lord Jesus Christ, is accountable to God for living a life separated from sin and characterized by the fruit of the Spirit. It is his responsibility to contribute by word and deed to the universal spread of the Gospel.

VII. At the end of the age the bodies of the dead shall be raised. The righteous shall enter into full possession of eternal bliss in the presence of God, and the wicked shall be condemned to eternal death."[12]

Given the central importance of the seminary's Basis of Faith, its founding vision and its Statement of Mission in providing the institution with a clear sense of its identity and purpose, one might assume that such missional clarity would inevitably persist.[13] Such

12. *Gordon-Conwell Theological Seminary Catalog 2002–2003* (So. Hamilton, MA: published by the seminary, 2002), 7.

13. Indeed, following the adoption of the Statement of Mission, President

confidence, sadly, is rarely rewarded. As historian George M. Marsden has suggested in his pioneering 1996 study of American higher education, the more familiar pattern in higher education seems to have been the virtually inexorable drift away from founding principles—what, in his subtitle, he spoke of as a movement "from Protestant establishment to established nonbelief."[14] Perhaps this is what the drafters of the seminary's Statement of Mission had in mind when they warned that Gordon-Conwell's "usefulness as a center of Christian learning would be vitiated and its relationship to the broader evangelical movement jeopardized" if the "twin convictions" of "the abiding truth of God's written Word and the centrality of Christ's saving work" should ever be "weakened" since they ever remain "the *sine qua non* for a coherent and effective educational program."[15]

Cooley established a Task Force (chaired by George Ensworth) to draft a Community Life Statement for the purpose of ensuring that the commitments of the seminary's new Statement of Mission were reflected in every aspect of community life.

14. George M. Marsden, *The Soul of the American University: Fro Protestant Establishment to Established Nonbelief* (New York: Oxford University Press, 1996). See also George M. Marsden and Bradley J. Longfield, *The Secularization of the Academy* (New York: Oxford University Press, 1992).

15. *The Mission of Gordon-Conwell Theological Seminary,* "Commentary," 3.

CHAPTER VIII

Expanding into Charlotte

It wasn't raining when Noah built the ark.[1]

—HOWARD RUFF, ECONOMIST

TUITION-DRIVEN INSTITUTIONS LIKE GORDON-CONWELL tend to be even more reliant upon a steady and reliable flow of new students than are those with substantial endowments or financially successful graduates. Consequently, new degree programs, new delivery systems, more comfortable accommodations, and new services are often developed to attract potential students. These produce new pressures on the budget, to be sure, but many believe that such expenses will ultimately be offset by additional growth.

Among Gordon-Conwell's most significant initiatives in addressing these kinds of concerns has been the establishment of branch campuses. Gordon-Conwell Theological Seminary—Charlotte, North Carolina, established in 1992, helped not only to enlarge the seminary's overall student population but it also expanded the seminary's ministry to a whole new region of the country.

1. Quotation by Howard Ruff taken from Jim Broughton, "It Wasn't Raining When Noah Built the Ark," in *W&G Today* (July 25, 2013).

The Charlotte Campus

"North Carolina is growing at a dramatic pace," concluded a Brookings Institution study in 2000, "in population, in jobs, and in land consumption." During the 1990s alone, the study found, more than a million new residents had entered the state. Drawn by its scenic beauty, job market, and "quality of life," in fact, tens of thousands had already begun making North Carolina their new home throughout the 1980s—enabling the state to become the sixth fastest growing region of the country.[2] As a student of such trends, President Cooley was well aware of these patterns and their implications for theological education. He was also aware that in Charlotte, North Carolina's largest city, no theological seminary had yet been established.[3] He also knew that if Gordon-Conwell ever decided to expand its physical presence beyond New England, Charlotte would certainly be among the most desirable places to do so.[4]

However, the first serious discussions of such a possibility did not take place until the summer of 1989 in a city nearly nine thousand miles from either Boston or Charlotte. The International

2. "Adding it Up: Growth Trends and Policies in North Carolina," a report prepared for the Z. Smith Reynolds Foundation by the Brookings Institution Center on Urban and Metropolitan Policy, July, 2000, 1–2.

3. Since the founding of Gordon-Conwell Theological Seminary in Charlotte, of course, several additional theological schools have been established.

4. During meetings with seminary graduates, in a series of ten alumni gatherings that President Cooley hosted in 1987, the need for a regionally-based campus was frequently raised as a possibility.

Congress on World Evangelization, known more popularly as Lausanne II, was meeting in the city of Manila in the Philippines during the month of July that year. In attendance at that gathering were the three men who, in the providence of God, would plant the seeds that would eventually lead to the establishment of a campus in the very heart of the American South: namely, Bob Cooley, Leighton Ford, and David Chadwick.[5]

Evangelist Leighton Ford, Longtime Trustee

Although three years of further conversation, feasibility studies and careful analysis would pass before their dream became a reality, the seed that had been planted in Manila had clearly taken root.[6] And by 1992, following the official approval for a campus

5. Robert J. Mayer, "Gordon-Conwell—Charlotte and Theological Education: Its History in Light of Emerging Trends," *Africanus Journal*, Vol. 8, No. 1 (April 2016), 39–48. David Chadwick was then the pastor of Forest Hill Church in Charlotte; Leighton Ford, the well-known evangelist, was a longtime member of the seminary's Board of Trustees; and Bob Cooley was then president of Gordon-Conwell Theological Seminary.

6. After careful deliberation, the Gordon-Conwell Theological Seminary

in Charlotte by the seminary's Board of Trustees, those tender roots had been transplanted in the rich soil of Forest Hill Church in Charlotte where over the next four years the young institution continued to grow and flourish. Classes were held on the congregation's spacious campus—beginning with a course in the Greek language taught by Professor Rollin Grams—and a library was established within one of the congregation's picturesque buildings.[7]

Forest Hill Church in Charlotte, North Carolina

---

faculty voted twenty-three to three in favor of establishing a campus in Charlotte.

7. Office space was also rented near the South Park Mall to house the staff and residential faculty. Ken Swetland, then serving as Associate Dean under Sid DeWaal, made numerous trips from Hamilton to Charlotte to teach and to help oversee the development of the new campus. He made so many trips, in fact, that his wife Anne began telling friends (with a twinkle in her eye) that Ken was away again visiting his "mistress named Charlotte!" For a fuller understanding of the development of the Charlotte campus, readers may wish to consult the author's oral history interviews with President Robert E. Cooley (10/16/2012), Evangelist Leighton Ford (2/21/2013), Charlotte Dean Wayne Goodwin (11/16/2012), Charlotte Dean Timothy Laniak (2/19/2013); Charlotte Dean Sidney Bradley (10/17/2012), and Administrative Assistant Patricia Nielsen (2/19/2013) in GMR Papers housed at Gordon-Conwell Theological Seminary.

For the new venture to be a success, however, President Cooley knew he would need to appoint the right Dean. Among those under consideration was Wayne Goodwin, then a member of the faculty of Asbury Theological Seminary. The two men spent a day together, as Dr. Goodwin described the process, talking about theological education in general, on which Wayne had written his doctoral thesis, and the president's specific vision for the new campus in Charlotte. By the end of the day, President Cooley knew he had found the person he needed. After confirmation by the faculty and board, Charlotte's new Executive Dean was officially installed. "Although your title is Executive Dean," President Cooley reminded his new colleague, "you will often need to function much like a president" since I cannot be present on campus all the time. Meanwhile, "you will have my full trust and support."[8]

Dean Wayne Goodwin

With President Cooley's continuing support, Dean Goodwin tackled his new responsibilities with characteristic energy and careful attention to detail. Determined to build an authentic "adult education model" of graduate theological education, he set

8. Oral history interview with Wayne Goodwin, October 16, 2012, GMR Papers housed at Gordon-Conwell Theological Seminary.

out to appoint a faculty, construct a working curriculum, prepare the necessary facilities, recruit new students, and secure sufficient financial resources to move the project forward.[9] From the beginning, most of the classes were offered on evenings and weekends so that working adults both within the Charlotte community and throughout North Carolina and the adjoining states could take classes and work toward one of the degrees that were offered.[10] The new seminary also gave special attention to the integration of theory and practice not only within its regular curricular offerings but also through its required twice-yearly integrative seminars, its creative community events, and its regular times of community worship. The Charlotte program also committed itself to what it liked to call a "pilgrim model," in partnership with several Charlotte-area churches, in which its classes were held in congregational facilities rather than in a facility of its own. Although growth in both faculty and student numbers eventually made its reliance on even the largest of Charlotte's facilities impracticable—and the building of its own campus a necessity—the seminary never abandoned its sense of connectedness with the churches of North Carolina.[11]

9. For a fuller description of the "adult education model" see Robert J. Mayer, "Gordon-Conwell—Charlotte and Theological Education: Its History in Light of Emerging Trends," *Africanus Journal*, Vol. 8, No. 1 (April 2016), 39–48; and Christine E. Blair, "Understanding Adult Learners: Challenges for Theological Education," *Theological Education* 34 (1997) 17–20.

10. Although a growing number of one-week intensive classes, hybrid and online classes and evening classes have been added over the years, the weekend classes (Friday evenings and Saturdays) remain a prominent part of the curricular offerings.

11. During its first four years, the seminary held its classes and kept its library at Forest Hill Church. Although its administrative offices and eventually its library holdings were moved into rented space, for more than a decade the classes continued to be held in local churches and in other facilities including the board room at SIM International. The seminary moved onto its present campus on Choate Circle in October of 2003. See also "Our Legacy, Our Future: Looking Ahead to the Next Decade" (Charlotte: by the Seminary, 2013).

A typical Charlotte Class

Although Dean Goodwin and his talented Administrative Assistant, Patricia Nielsen, deserve much of the credit for the design and implementation of Gordon-Conwell in Charlotte, his four successors have all made significant contributions in shaping the southern campus. David Wells, who succeeded Dean Goodwin in 1998, helped to deepen the connection between the Charlotte campus and the rest of the institution.[12] Sid Bradley, who became Dean in 2000, not only presided over the construction of Charlotte's first permanent campus buildings in 2003 but he also helped to establish "the first Christian counseling program in North Carolina to be licensed to train graduates for the Licensed Professional Counselor (LPC) and Marriage and Family (MFT) certifications" and he helped to usher in the new Master of Arts in Christian Leadership degree program (MACL) that is currently directed by Professor Rodney Cooper.[13] Dean Bradley's gracious

12. "Wells Appointed Academic Dean at Charlotte," *Hilltop*, Vol. 10, No. 1 (Summer 1998), 1.

13. Robert J. Mayer, "Gordon-Conwell—Charlotte and Theological

southern style and educational savvy brought fresh stability and focus to the young campus.

Dean Sid Bradley

When Dean Bradley decided to return to the classroom in 2008, Timothy Laniak was appointed to succeed him. In addition to successfully guiding the Charlotte campus through a period of economic depression, Dean Laniak helped to renew the seminary's emphasis on biblical literacy, on lay education and (with the valuable assistance of Professor Steve Klipowicz) on ministerial formation. In 2016, Professor Donald Fairbairn was appointed to succeed Dean Laniak in Charlotte's Office of Academic Dean.

Education: Its History in Light of Emerging Trends," *Africanus Journal*, Vol. 8, No. 1 (April 2016), 44.

With training in Patristic Studies, Dean Fairbairn has taken up his new responsibilities with characteristic competence and energy.

Although the number of residential faculty based in Charlotte has continued to grow, the longstanding practice of sharing faculty across campus settings has also continued to enrich Charlotte's programs. While it is certainly true that the seminary's main campus in Hamilton has provided most of the commuting faculty members for the other campuses, the presence of colleagues from those settings has also become a familiar feature in Hamilton.

Hamilton Faculty who have Commuted to Charlotte[14]

"The Charlotte campus has produced over 1,000 graduates," historian Bob Mayer has observed, serving "in Christian vocations in the American Southeast and throughout the world. Many of these students have embraced the call of pastoral ministry. Others are serving in counseling and mental health practices. Still others serve in Christian organizations and in world missions. Some have even sensed God's call to remain in their professional vocation (law, medicine, accounting, and others) and serve Christ in their original calling. Some have pursued further education including doctoral studies. And some have become writers and authors

14. Some of the Hamilton-based faculty who commuted regularly to Charlotte to teach courses: (left to right) Professors Kaminski, Keazirian, Cooper, Gibson, Polischuk, Champa, Isaac, Swetland, Pendleton, Currie, Adams, Rosell, D. Petter, Borgman, Davis, T. Petter, and Niehaus.

whose work has benefited the cause of Christ through biblically grounded literature of various forms."[15]

Charlotte Faculty in 2018[16]

In December of 2012, the Charlotte community paused to celebrate its twentieth anniversary and to express its gratitude to God for His abundant blessings over the seminary's first two decades. The speaker for that gathering was its first Executive Dean, Wayne Goodwin, the leader that Bob Cooley had appointed back in 1992.[17] Focusing his reflections around three points of reference,

15. Robert J. Mayer, "Gordon-Conwell—Charlotte and Theological Education: Its History in Light of Emerging Trends," *Africanus Journal*, Vol. 8, No. 1 (April 2016), 48.

16. Photo of the Charlotte faculty in 2018. First row (left to right): Carolina Benitez (Counseling), Pam Davis (Counseling), Nicole Martin (Ministry and Leadership), Tim Laniak (Old Testament), Don Fairbairn (Academic Dean), Rodney Cooper (Leadership and Ministry), SeJin Koh (Cooley Center Director and Korean Studies). Second Row: Rollin Grams (New Testament), Bob Mayer (Head Librarian), Brent Burdick (Missions), Gerry Wheaton (New Testament), Cathy McDowell (Old Testament), Vickey Maclin (Counseling Administration), Chris Cook (Counseling). Photo arranged by Bob Mayer and taken by Jonathan Parker from Media Services.

17. Wayne Goodwin, "Gordon-Conwell—Charlotte: 20th Anniversary

he reminded his listeners of what he called the "programs," the "presence" and the "people" that have "characterized this remarkable institution" throughout its first twenty years. The "programs," what has been called "the Charlotte Model," can be seen in "its highly successful counseling program," in its unique "Mentored Ministry" program, in its pioneering uses of technology and in its innovative approach to the development of leadership. Funded by generous grants from foundations such as the Lilly Endowment along with the personal generosity of friends such as Virginia Snoddy, these cutting-edge programs have helped to give a unique flavor to the educational offerings on the Charlotte campus. Undergirding these programs has been the development of a campus that both supports and enhances the work they represent. "Our mission remains the same: a passionate commitment to the highest levels of theological scholarship, a thoughtful Evangelicalism, and a focused effort to serve the Church with excellence and distinction," wrote President Emeritus Robert E. Cooley, chairman of the Charlotte Building Campaign, but "now is the time to expand the boundaries in theological education at Gordon-Conwell Theological Seminary—Charlotte." This, he continued, will require "new efforts to educate and to pursue transformational learning, to create new spaces for community-building activity, and to provide new forms of learning resources through digital technology and global partnerships."[18] Among the most exciting of these innovations has been the launching of "Digital Live" initiative that simultaneously brings the live classroom experience to students around the globe.[19]

Presentation," delivered on December 7, 2012. Copy in the GMR Papers housed at the seminary.

18. "A Letter from Dr. Robert Cooley, President Emeritus of Gordon-Conwell," in "Our Legacy, Our Future: Serving the Church with Excellence and Innovation: Expanding the Boundaries of Theological Education," published by the seminary for Gordon-Conwell Theological Seminary: Charlotte. Copy in GMR Papers housed at the seminary. Included are drawings of the new "Hall of the Bible," the "Hall of Worship and Spiritual Formation," and the "Hall of Global Mission."

19. "Digital Live," by means of high-speed internet connections, provides students connecting to the course at a distance to receive the same teaching

The Robert and Eileen Cooley Chapel on the Charlotte Campus

These buildings and programs, Dean Goodwin also reminded his listeners on that twentieth anniversary, would not be possible without the "presence" of the Holy Spirit guiding "in every aspect of the process" and providing, with the gracious cooperation of the Sudan Interior Mission (SIM), the twenty acres of land on which the campus now stands. What you may not know, Goodwin continued, "is that the faculty and staff came to this property and mowed grass and cut weeds and put up a sign 'The Future Home of Gordon-Conwell Theological Seminary'" after walking "around this property" and praying "that it would be used to honor God. As we walked we prayed and as we prayed it all began to fall into place and today you are recipients of those prayers and the dedication of all of these early pioneers who prayed this campus into existence."

---

through live feeds of the professor and his/her presentations as well as student discussions. Students are able to interact live with the professor, with the other students in the classroom and with other students connecting from around the world through live video, chat, group project work and other features.

Classroom on the Charlotte Campus

At the heart of the story, as told by Dean Goodwin that day, are the people—indeed, the people who made the Charlotte campus a reality. Citing the contributions of colleagues such as Sid Bradley, Tim Laniak, Robert Mayer, Rollin Grams, Donald Keeney, Joel Harlow, Steve Klipowitz, Judy Smith, Trish King, Tim Myrick, Garth Rosell, Virginia and Mark Snoddy, Lance Nelson, Jeremy Long, Scott Smith, David Chadwick, David Rogers, Joe Cathy, Ron Riley, Sue Moore, Joanne Davidson, Susan Sloan, Miller Byne, and so many more, Dean Goodwin reserved his highest accolades for the true founder of Gordon-Conwell Theological Seminary—Charlotte. "Effective leaders," Goodwin opined, have the "discernment" to "see what others cannot see" and the ability "to cast a vision" and "lead others to accomplish the vision." Such a leader, he continued, is with us today. "Will you join me in recognizing the one who will always be my president, my colleague, a leader of leaders, and most importantly, my friend—Dr. Robert E.

Cooley. Bob, this is your day." [20] Visitors to the Charlotte campus will be reminded of the special bond that has developed between Gordon-Conwell's third campus and its second president when they note that the chapel is named in honor of Bob and Eileen Cooley.

The Harold Lindsell Library on the Charlotte Campus

Visitors to the campus will also be reminded of the important place within the seminary's history that has been occupied by Harold Lindsell, the first Chair of Gordon-Conwell Theological Seminary's Board of Trustees. For nearly a quarter of a century, Lindsell presided over the meetings of both the full board and its executive committee. Charlotte's Lindsell Library is a fitting tribute to his many years of service to the school.

The seminary's first library, as we have learned, was built on the Hamilton campus and named after Burton Goddard, a former academic dean who served as the seminary's first librarian. In 1973, Goddard retired from his responsibilities as head librarian and was asked to serve as the "Librarian Consultant." Robert C. Dvorak was then appointed as Goddard Library's Director and

20. Wayne Goodwin, "Gordon-Conwell—Charlotte: 20th Anniversary Presentation," December 7, 2012, 1–6.

Head Librarian and Ken Umenhofer assumed the title of Associate Director of the Library. The new \$1,500,000 Goddard Library, opened in time for the Fall Semester in 1971, housed some 57,000 catalogued volumes and room for nearly 100,000 more.

**The Seminary's Second Head Librarian
Robert C. Dvorak**[21]

In addition to the "two large amphitheater-type classrooms and a score of faculty offices" that were included within Goddard Library, a "rare book room," of sufficient size to "house not only the many individual rare books but Gordon-Conwell archives and special collections," enabled the seminary to properly house the Edward Payson Vining Collection (jointly owned by the seminary and Gordon College), several hundred rare Bibles, a number of seventeenth- and eighteenth-century Puritan publications and

21. Robert C. Dvorak served the seminary with genuine distinction in a variety of key faculty and administrative roles during his lengthy tenure on the Hamilton campus: much beloved as a teacher, he also served for many years as Head Librarian and from time to time as Associate Dean, Acting Dean, committee chair, choir director, principal author of an Accreditation Self-Study, pianist/organist, to mention a few.

approximately 2,000 Assyro-Babylonian volumes from the library of Samuel A. B. Mercer.[22] By the time of the 2005 accreditation visit, the Goddard Library had expanded its holdings to more than two-hundred-thousand books, some twenty thousand bound periodicals, nearly a hundred computer databases, almost a thousand periodicals and hundreds of manuscripts. In addition, it had added three enormously valuable collections: the Harold John Ockenga Papers, the Adventual Collection and (thanks to the generosity of Professor William Nigel Kerr) hundreds of editions of John Bunyan's *Pilgrim's Progress.*

22. Descriptions taken from the *Gordon-Conwell Theological Seminary Catalog* for 1974/75, pages 14–15.

Bob Mayer, Head Librarian (2006-present)

Although two additional libraries are now housed in Boston and Jacksonville, the seminary's second largest library is located on the Charlotte campus. The Lindsell Library, as it is known, not only played a key role in the establishment of the Carolinas Theological Library Consortium (CTLC), an organization that has greatly enhanced the resources for theological education in the southeast, but it also co-hosted a meeting of the American Theological Library Association in 2013. Overseeing all four of the seminary's libraries is Robert Mayer, who was first appointed in 1997 to serve as the Director of the Harold Lindsell Library in Charlotte and was subsequently appointed to serve as the seminary's Head Librarian in 2006. Under his leadership, the libraries on all four campuses have been working to preserve and expand the library's overall holdings, to provide access to new databases such as the recently added Digital Theological Library (DTL) and to keep up with the dramatic technological changes that are quite literally changing the shape and direction of educational libraries. Special attention is also being given to the preservation, cataloging, and use of a growing number of archival collections.

CHAPTER IX

Building Bridges to the Church

Education is all a matter of building bridges[1]

—RALPH ELLISON

"THE SEMINARY," AS THE Statement of Mission repeatedly asserts, is "a training partner with the Church so that what is learned on campus may be complemented by the spiritual nurture and the exercise of ministry available through the Church."[2] But exactly how—in the often frenetic ebb and flow of institutional life—is that mission to be accomplished? And how—given the heavy demands that graduate theological education places upon faculty and students alike—can genuine and constructive bridges be built between the seminary and the church?

An answer to those important questions began to take shape during the 1980–81 academic year in a series of conversations between the Academic Dean and Carlyle Saylor.[3] By the autumn of

1. Quotation from Ralph Ellison taken from a Rebecca Darling blog (November 8, 2011) on blogs.cornell.edu

2. *The Mission of Gordon-Conwell Theological Seminary* (So. Hamilton, MA: by the Seminary, 1983), 3.

3. Dave Keazirian, "Proposal for Institute for Evangelical Studies Goes to

1983, with the strong support of President Cooley and a thorough vetting by both the faculty and the administration, the idea for an institute designed to enable more regular and productive connections between seminary and church began to take the form of a written proposal.[4] The proposal for the establishment of an "Institute for Evangelical Studies," as it was initially known, was then approved by vote of the faculty and presented to the Academic Affairs Committee of the seminary's Board of Trustees for consideration on October 7, 1983. Upon the committee's favorable recommendation, the proposal was forwarded to the full Board of Trustees for its review and approval at their midyear gathering in 1984. Only one significant change was added to the document when it was endorsed with enthusiasm by the board. The new initiative, they decreed, would be renamed "The Harold John Ockenga Institute" in honor of the seminary's first president. "The Ockenga Institute," commented President Cooley, "is a fitting way to honor and continue Dr. Ockenga's distinguished ministry to New England and the world."[5] Indeed, the Institute has remained the only "structure" on any of our four campus settings that bears the founder's name.[6]

In a news release announcing the establishment of the Harold John Ockenga Institute, President Cooley noted that through "centers for church renewal, World missions and contemporary issues" the new initiative would seek to "develop courses, seminars, conferences and research activities involving scholars and

the Trustees," *The Gordon-Conwell Trib*, Vol. 10, No. 1 (October 27, 1983), 1. "The idea for the Institute," Saylor remarked to the writer of the article, "was conceived within the mind of Garth Rosell nearly three years ago."

4. Carlyle Saylor, "A Proposal: The Institute for Evangelical Studies," copy in the GMR Papers housed at the seminary.

5. Michelle S. Mohney, "The Harold John Ockenga Institute," *Contact*, Vol. 14, No. 2 (Winter 1985), 12; and "Memorandum to Administration/Faculty/Staff/Students" (February 4, 1985) from Robert E. Cooley, President in the GMR Papers housed at the seminary.

6. Although one of the roads on the Hamilton campus has been named in his honor, no other program or building on any of the seminary's campuses carries the Ockenga name.

practitioners from many fields." It is, he continued, to be a "delivery vehicle," helping to make "the educational resources of the seminary available to persons in many walks of life." So that the institute would not prove to "be a drain" on the seminary's budget and "on the traditional programs of theological education at the seminary," its founders were all in agreement that the cost of all its centers and programs would be covered either by endowment funds raised for that purpose or through earnings generated by the centers. In short, the institute was to be financially self-sufficient.[7] Soon—through the exceptional generosity of donors like the Shoemakers, the Mocklers, the Baraca-Philathea board members, and others—literally millions of endowment dollars were provided to enable the young centers to flourish and grow. Without these visionary leaders, the seminary's new initiative to link seminary and church would never have become a reality.[8]

The Mission of the Ockenga Institute

"The twin concerns" that brought the Harold John Ockenga Institute into existence, as Saylor liked to express it, "are the renewal of the Church and the evangelization of the world." Indeed, the new institute should be understood as "an administrative and educational umbrella" under which the seminary's "Statement of Mission" can be brought to bear "on planning for the future of Gordon-Conwell."[9] Or to shift the metaphor from the umbrella to the bridge, as Saylor often did, the institute was designed to serve as one of the seminary's most important means of building bridges between the seminary and the church. Its record in doing so is truly impressive.[10]

7. Copies of internal correspondence and the official news release can be found in the GMR Papers housed at the seminary.

8. Documents relating to some of this remarkable generosity can found in the GMR Papers housed at Gordon-Conwell Theological Seminary.

9. Dave Keazirian, "Proposal for Institute for Evangelical Studies Goes to the Trustees," *The Gordon-Conwell Trib*, Vol. 10, No. 1 (October 27, 1983), 1.

10. For a fuller discussion of the Ockenga Institute, see *Ockenga*

During its first two decades, a variety of centers, dozens of programs, scores of educational opportunities and numerous conferences, round-tables, and workshops helped "to make the rich educational resources of the Seminary available" and accessible to literally thousands of pastors, missionaries, and lay leaders around the globe.[11] Equally impressive were the hundreds of pastors and lay Christian leaders from New England and beyond who regularly made their way to campus to attend one or another of the dozens of gatherings large and small that had become a familiar aspect of seminary life. "When I arrived on campus during the late 1970s," as one faculty member remarked, "I only rarely ran into anyone who was not a part of the seminary community. But now, thanks to the Ockenga Institute, it seems that there are new faces everywhere."

Connections, Vol. 5, No. 4 (Winter 2000); Contact magazine, Vol. 30, No. 1 (Summer 2000), 3–13, 20–21; and the author's interview with Carl and Avis Saylor (4/12/2013) in the GMR Papers housed at Gordon-Conwell Theological Seminary.

11. "The Ockenga Vision: Celebrating 15 Years of Ministry Partnership," Gordon-Conwell Theological Seminary Contact, Vol. 30, No. 1 (Summer 2000), 1; and the Ockenga Connections: 15th Anniversary Edition, Vol. 5, No. 4 (Winter 2000). For more recent statistics see David Horn, "Ockenga Institute by the Numbers: Making an Impact for the Kingdom," GMR Papers housed at Gordon-Conwell Theological Seminary.

Professor Carl Saylor, First Director of the Institute[12]

From its founding in 1985, the Ockenga Institute has been guided by the four core values that form the foundation of Gordon-Conwell's larger mission: namely, the spread of the gospel around the globe; the renewal of the church; the transformation of culture in every segment of society through Christian influence as "salt and light;" and the rigorous training for ministry of new generations of Christian leaders with a thorough education and "a burning love for Jesus."[13] It is that vision, in fact, that led to the establishment—under the broad umbrella of the Harold John Ockenga Institute—of the J. Christy Wilson Center for World Missions, the Shoemaker Center for Church Renewal, the Mockler Center for Marketplace Ministry, the Center for the Study of Global Christianity, the Haddon W. Robinson Center for Preaching,

12. Carlyle Saylor served as Director from 1985 to 1987. He was succeeded by Garth M. Rosell (1987–2004), David Horn (2004–17) and David Currie (2017-present)

13. *Contact* magazine, "The Ockenga Vision: Celebrating 15 Years of Ministry Partnership," Vol. 30, No. 1 (Summer 2000) and "The Ockenga Institute: Mission, Strategy and Structure," in the GMR Papers housed at the seminary.

the Center for Christian Youth, the Ockenga Ministry Resource Center, the New England Research Center, the Cooley Center for the Study of Early Christianity, the Center for the Development of Evangelical Leadership, and the Baraca-Philathea Center. These centers and the programs they have overseen have helped to transform the seminary community from a relatively isolated group of academics to a mission-driven community of global educators.

Barry and Paula Corey

In addressing those who had gathered in April of 2004 to celebrate the institute's twentieth anniversary and the transfer of leadership from its second director to its third, Barry Corey, the seminary's academic dean, described the twenty-year process that had forged what he called an "incubator for new ideas" known as the Ockenga Institute, the institution's "fledgling, innovative, educational laboratory," into one of the most important missional structures in the seminary. Few could have imagined during its early years, he continued, that such a tiny "seed" would eventually grow into "a thriving Institute" that would enable "the seminary's educational resources to be available to local churches and likewise for local churches' resources to benefit the seminary." The Institute, by God's grace, had become—to borrow Dean Corey's words—"a formidable arm of the Seminary."[14]

Indeed, the impact of the Ockenga Institute has been enormous. As Dave Horn, its third director, noted in an "Ockenga Institute by the Numbers" report in 2015, the institute's various centers and programs have touched thousands of men and women in more than one-hundred countries around the globe providing them with educational resources that they could not have accessed otherwise—from specialized training programs and free courses to preaching aids, distance education opportunities, workshops, and seminars. Only eternity will fully reveal the immense impact that the Ockenga Institute has had both on campus and around the globe.[15]

Dave Horn, Third Director of the Institute

14. Barry Corey, "A Letter" (Wednesday, April 28, 2004), on the occasion of the 20th anniversary of the founding of the Ockenga Institute, the retirement of Garth M. Rosell as Director (1987–2004) and the appointment of David Horn as its third Director (2004–2015). Copy in the GMR Papers housed at Gordon-Conwell Theological Seminary.

15. Dave Horn, "Ockenga Institute by the Numbers," 2015 report. Copy in GMR Papers housed at the seminary.

None of these remarkable programs would have been possible, of course, without the commitment, dedication and hard work of a gifted staff. Across the institute's more than thirty years, God has been pleased to call dozens of dedicated women and men into leadership for the dozens and dozens of programs that took shape in the various centers. And in the process—through its regular planning retreats, social gatherings and the remarkable "people skills" of Dave Horn—the staff was forged into a visionary, mission-centered and closely-knit team of colleagues in ministry.

Ockenga Institute Staff in 2000[16]

16. On its 15th anniversary in 2000, the Ockenga Institute staff numbered 25. Pictured in front row (l to r): Bob Barnett, Anne Bacher, Garth Rosell (Director), Tammy Wise, Holly McKenzie, Sarah Samuelson, Edie Finnell, Dana Hess, Terri Tanaka and Barb Fischer. In back row (l to r): Kent Edwards, Dave Horn, David Eastman, Curt Wanner, Ann Olson, Will Messenger and Cory Hartman. Not pictured: Meredith Armbrust, Doug Birdsall, Jeff Brinkman, Chris Castaldo, Aaron Dowdell, Linford Fisher, Jay Gromek, and Melissa Johnson. Photo from *Ockenga Connections*, Vol. 5, No. 4 (Winter 2000), 3.

Mission
The mission of the Ockenga Institute is to help make the seminary's educational resources available to the church and to help make the church's educational resources available to the seminary.

Strategy
The Ockenga Institute seeks to accomplish its mission through the work of its six ministry centers, its various educational programs and its research projects.

Structure
The Ockenga Institute is structured as an umbrella organization—seeking to enhance communication, coordinate activities and reduce costs in its various interrelated centers and programs through shared personnel, expertise and equipment.

Pastors Builders Series	Semlink Online	Mockler Adult Education Classes
International Teaching	Pastors Wilderness	Biblical Languages, Semlink
Practical Faith in Marketplace	Marketplace Mentored Ministry	Mockler Panel Discussions
Pastors Forum	Baraca-Philathea History	Chapel Tapes
Mockler Distinguished Lectures	Missionaries-in-Residence	Wilson Lunch Forums
Christian StudiesSeminar	Timothy Project	Ministry Partner's Conversations
Ockenga Summer Conference	World Discovery Weekends	Mockler Conversation's
Real Ministry Immersion	Mockler DMIN Programs	Scholars-in-Residence
Global Focus Evenings	Dimensions of Faith	Diploma Program
Spurgeon Sabbatical	Mockler Discussion Groups	New England Partners Survey
Brown Bag Sabbatical	Holy Land Tour	Ockenga Writer's Conference
New England 8 Traits Research	Pastor's Conversations	Faith Builders Series
Mockler Scholar	Mockler Faculty Lunch	Ockenga Connections
Paul Tom's Lectureship	Youth Mentoring	Mockler Conferences
Spiritual Heritage Tours	Boston Plunge	

Taking its cue from the Ockenga vision, the Institute's first three centers were the Center for World Mission (designed by Professor J. Christy Wilson, Jr. and later named in his honor), the Shoemaker Center for Church Renewal (named in honor of Albert and Merdie Shoemaker whose multi-million dollar endowment made it possible); and the Mockler Center for Marketplace Ministry (named in honor of Colman and Joanna Mockler whose generous endowment made its ministry possible). Other centers followed, including the Baraca-Philathea Center, dedicated to the task of encouraging biblical literacy; and the Center for the Study of Global Christianity, directed by Professor Todd Johnson and committed to the task of continuing the internationally-recognized demographic studies and publications that the legendary Dr. Barrett had begun many years before; and the Haddon Robinson Center for Preaching, named in honor of Professor Haddon Robinson and directed for many years by his colleague, Scott Gibson, and more recently has been co-directed by his colleagues Jeff Arthurs and Matthew Kim and with Patricia Batten serving as Associate Director.[17] Taken together, these centers and their programs have quite literally "put Gordon-Conwell Theological Seminary" on the global map.[18]

All of these remarkable centers (along with the dozens of programs to which each has given birth) deserve far more attention, of course, than the pages in this relatively modest history will allow. The Wilson Center, for example, through programs such as the Overseas Missions Practicum enabled the seminary to fulfill the sixth article of its Mission Statement through programs that help to "develop in students a vision for God's redemptive work throughout the world and to formulate strategies that will lead to effective missions, evangelism and discipleship."[19] The Mockler Center, under a succession of outstanding directors, made it possible for the seminary to fulfill its commitment to article five of the seminary's Mission through its efforts "to provide leadership and educational resources for shaping an effective evangelical presence in Church and society."[20] The Baraca-Philathea Center, with its encouragement of biblical literacy, helped the seminary to fulfill its mandate

17. Scott M. Gibson, who provided outstanding leadership as Director of the Center for Preaching, was appointed David E. Garland Professor of Preaching and Director of the PhD Program in Preaching at Baylor University's Truett Seminary in 2018. His wife, Rhonda, also served with distinction for many years as Gordon-Conwell's Director of the Alumni Office.

18. For the larger story of their programs and leadership, see *Contact* magazine, Vol. 30, No. 1 (Summer 2000) and *Ockenga Institute Connections*, Vol. 5, No. 4 (Winter 2000).

19. Quotations are taken from "The Mission of Gordon-Conwell Theological Seminary," 4.

20. Directing the Mockler Center have been such gifted leaders as Pete Hammond, Will Messenger, David Gill and its current director, Kenneth Barnes.

in article one "of encouraging students to become knowledgeable of God's inerrant Word." The Shoemaker Center, through its encouragement of spiritual renewal, helped the seminary make good on its commitment to foster an "experiential knowledge of God in Christ" that is evidenced in "their character, outlook, conduct, relationships and involvement in society." The Haddon Robinson Center for Preaching helped the seminary to fulfill its promise in articles one and three of encouraging students to become "skilled in ministry" and competent in the "interpretation, proclamation and application" of God's Word within "the contemporary world." And the Center for the Study of Global Christianity, under the able leadership of Todd Johnson and his team of researchers, helped the seminary "to maintain academic excellence in the highest tradition of Christian scholarship," to provide "educational resources for shaping an effective evangelical presence in Church and society" and to "develop in students a vision for God's redemptive work throughout the world." Without these centers and programs, in fact, it is difficult to imagine how the seminary would have been able to fulfill a wide array of commitments that the institution has made through the adoption of its Statement of Mission.

A core commitment for all of the centers and their programs has been a recognition that the institute's major responsibility is to support, undergird, enrich, and extend the primary educational mission of the seminary. Rather than replace the work of the faculty, the Ockenga Institute has always seen its task as ancillary to and supportive of the work of the teaching faculty. Nowhere has this commitment been more evident than in one of the institute's most important, innovative, and successful programs—namely, the initiative originally known as the "Independent Studies Program" and later renamed the Semlink Program. Designed to serve three important functions—namely, (1) to make the basic courses offered on campus available to those who were unable to access them on campus; (2) to serve as a recruitment vehicle by allowing prospective students to experience actual seminary courses (taught by the seminary's own faculty) before arriving on campus; and (3) to enable students on campus to have sufficient flexibility in scheduling courses so as to complete their degrees in a timely manner—the program soon became the seminary's most effective "feeder system" for prospective students and it did so while adding significant revenue, in excess of program costs, to the seminary's annual budgets.

Begun in 1987 under the leadership of Robert Freeman, Semlink was regularly revised and updated to keep the lectures current and to make sure that the program conformed to accreditation standards. Under the leadership of Dave Horn, who became its director in 1999, Semlink was updated regularly and its course offerings were significantly expanded.[21] "Previously, students were permitted to take four [Semlink] courses for the MDiv and MA degrees," Horn reported, but "they are now permitted to take 10 for the MDiv and 6 for the MA degrees. We are especially excited about our Semlink MDiv degree that allows students to take the first 10 of their courses in their place of ministry prior to arriving on campus."[22]

Students were equally enthused since the new program provided greater flexibility for on-campus students while enabling off-campus students, including pastors, missionaries, military chaplains, youth leaders, and others a workable structure within which they could pursue God's call in their life. "Through this program," wrote one prospective student, "I will be able to do the impossible—support a family, meet obligations, and transition to a new career" while following God's call in my life. Dozens and dozens of other prospective students echoed the same sentiment.

"We are particularly encouraged," remarked Dave Horn in announcing the newly updated program, "by the 28 new students" who are now officially enrolled in our Master of Divinity degree. It seems hardly a coincidence that the same issue of *Hilltop* magazine also announced that the seminary was experiencing a "record

21. "Faculty Approves New Independent Study Program," *Hilltop*, Vol. 1, No. 2 (April 1987), 3.

22. David Horn, "Semlink Program Officially Launched," in *Hilltop*, Vol. 11, No. 1 (Winter 1999), 11. The new name, "Semlink," was officially adopted in 1999.

enrollment." All of "the Gordon-Conwell campuses are experiencing high enrollment," the article reported. "The main campus in South Hamilton, Massachusetts has a current enrollment of 629 students, 202 of which are new students, a 12 percent increase over last year and a 15-year institution high." Moreover, the seminary's Boston campus "is up 50% from last year with a growing total student body of 198" and "at our campus in Charlotte, North Carolina" the fulltime-equivalent enrollment "has increased 76 percent from last year, with 209 registered students, and a fulltime equivalent of 79."

President Walt Kaiser

None of these developments would have been possible, of course, without the strong support of the seminary's presidents and their leadership teams. Indeed, from its earliest days, President Cooley's enthusiastic commitment to the project was absolutely essential and without his continued engagement, fund-raising, and encouragement the Ockenga Institute would never have become a reality. With the inauguration in 1997 of Walt Kaiser as the seminary's third president, it soon became apparent that the Ockenga Institute had been blessed with another strong advocate.[23] Not only did he continue the work that his predecessor had started but he further expanded the range of ministries in which the institute was engaged.

Nowhere was this more evident than it was in the institute's Center for Preaching. President Kaiser's profound commitment to the task of preparing men and women to "preach the Word" is the stuff of legend. Indeed, there could not have been a more appropriate tribute to his years of service here at the seminary than for the Board of Trustees to name the chapel on the Hamilton campus in

23. President Walter C. Kaiser, Jr., a distinguished Old Testament scholar, was inaugurated on October 9, 1997 at Boston's historic Park Street Church. See "Kaiser Inaugurated as Third President," *Gordon-Conwell Theological Seminary Hilltop*, Vol. 9, No. 2 (Fall 1997), 1 and following. A copy of the inauguration program can be found in the GMR Papers housed at the seminary.

his honor. For despite the frequent travel that called a busy president away from campus, President Kaiser was invariably present each and every Wednesday to preach in the chapel that bears his name. "We can't expect our students to recognize the importance of preaching," he once told this writer, "if we as leaders do not model and live by our commitment to its importance."

Marge and Walt Kaiser with Professors Pratico and Polischuk

In his inaugural acceptance speech in 1997, President Kaiser established preaching of the Word as the centerpiece in his vision for the seminary. "The starting place for our work," he declared like a prophet of old, "will not be in society, but in the church." The unique gift "that an evangelical seminary has to offer a church" is "the full declaration of the word of God. No famine is so pressing and no hunger so egregious as that of the hunger and famine for expository preaching of the word of God in all churches, evangelical or not! This condition must no longer persist if the Church is ever to be accounted as having any force worth paying any attention to in our society. Too long have the people of God had to fend for themselves or had to put up with the husks and leftovers of emaciated substitutions for the powerful word of the prophets and apostles. In lieu of the 'whole counsel of God,' all too many have had to make do with pop psychology, inexpert sociology, idealistic philosophies of one sort or another, while the culture continued to cry out, 'Is there no voice from God?'"[24]

Professor Alice Mathews with Haddon and Bonnie Robinson

"By God's help," President Kaiser concluded, "this deprivation will cease as a whole new generation of preachers, teachers, evangelists, and missionaries accept the challenge to end the famine of the word of God by boldly speaking that word into all the vacuums of modern life. That word is still the 'power of God' to everyone who believes; it still can split the hardest of issues in two, for it is a word from on high." With God's help, we will be "that institution that dares to take him and his word on its own terms."

24. Walter C. Kaiser, Jr., "The Evangelical Seminary of the Twenty-First Century: Text of the Inaugural Acceptance Speech presented by President Walter C. Kaiser, Jr. on October 9, 1997," in *Hilltop*, Vol. 9, No. 2 (Fall 1997), 2 and 11.

Nothing "is too hard for God. He is still calling individuals for his purposes. He is still calling out the best minds of our day to dedicate their lives to serving him body, soul and mind to the glory of his great name. And that word will cut through the issues, powers, and competitors of our day. May God help his Church to rise to what could be her finest hour ever."[25] The Center for Preaching, named in honor of Haddon Robinson, became one of the primary means of implementing this compelling vision. Along with the seminary's strong preaching department and President Kaiser's own example, it provided programmatic undergirding, to borrow the words of the seminary's Statement of Mission, in helping students to become competent in the "interpretation, proclamation and application" of God's Word "in the contemporary world."

Meeting of the Christian Thought Division

25. Kaiser, "The Evangelical Seminary of the Twenty-First Century," 11.

CHAPTER X

Facing Challenges

When everything seems to be going against you, remember that the airplane takes off against the wind, not with it.

—HENRY FORD

THEOLOGICAL SEMINARIES, LIKE OTHER institutions of higher education, must regularly contend with a variety of difficulties, challenges, and disruptions. Budget shortfalls, enrollment declines, student protests, breakdown of copy machines, curricular debates, office assignments, course load requirements, Wi-Fi connectivity, course reading lists, and dozens of additional concerns can disrupt and roil even the most bucolic of campus communities. Institutions like those who occupy them, it would seem, are "born to trouble as the sparks fly upward."[1]

Like most of its sister institutions, Gordon-Conwell Theological Seminary has faced its fair share of problems and challenges across the years—from occasional town/gown disagreements; or the angry confrontations that periodically erupt between members of the faculty, administration and board; or budget shortfalls

---

1. Book of Job, chapter five, verses six and seven (ESV)

that cause the dismissal of beloved colleagues; or serious issues of theological orthodoxy that seem to emerge from time to time. Some have been resolved with Christian grace. Others remain largely unresolved.

The challenges faced at Gordon-Conwell during its first half-century, in retrospect, have tended to cluster around four primary concerns: namely, student enrollment (either there are too many students or too few); shared governance (what are the appropriate roles played by faculty, administration and trustees); academic freedom (especially as it relates to the theological boundaries established by the seminary's statement of faith); and institutional mission and identity (with special reference to the seminary's founding vision and its statement of mission). We will examine each of these individually.

Student Enrollment

Evangelical seminaries, with rare exception, tend to be tuition driven. With relatively modest endowments, they keep an unusually sharp eye on enrollment trends and changing patterns. During the years between the seminary's founding in 1969 and its peak year for overall enrollment in 2006, the pattern generally was one of growth. However, between 2006 and 2018 the overall pattern has trended downward. While the reasons for these trends can be debated, the impact they have had on seminaries like Gordon-Conwell can hardly be ignored. Budgets, personnel decisions, institutional policies, advertising expenditures, building maintenance, travel expenditures, and scores of additional institutional decisions are affected by changes in the student population. However, too much growth in enrollment on the one hand or too sharp a decline in student numbers on the other almost always affects the general campus morale and the smooth functioning of the institution.

Some have turned to demographic trends to help explain such advances and declines in enrollment. Changing patterns, for example, from the shrinking of mainline denominations to the declining birth rates within certain segments of the population, are undoubtedly significant when evaluating enrollment trends. By themselves, however, they cannot fully explain why some seminaries are shrinking while others continue to grow. An ATS study on "Seminary Enrollment Trends" published by Tom Tanner and Eliza Smith Brown in 2015, reflects the surprising finding that while a number of seminaries are indeed declining, a substantial number of others are actually growing.[2]

Other analysts, quite rightly, have noted that the evangelical world itself has been changing—abandoning important aspects of its theological character and diminishing for some potential students both the need and desire for pursuing theological education. Indeed, as theologian David Wells has suggested, "some evangelical churches today are saying that they do not want a seminary trained pastor and some churches are training their own pastors."[3] Still others, seeking in particular an explanation for the recent decline in student numbers, have focused on the growing economic pressures faced by prospective students, arguing that graduate education has simply priced itself out of the market. College graduates, they rightly note, are often so burdened with undergraduate debt that they are either unwilling or unable to consider adding more.

Whatever the reasons for the enrollment decline, however, it would appear that perceived quality clearly matters in the process of selecting a place to study. As has been true for many years, prospective students still seem to be attracted to institutions with the strongest academic credentials (as reflected in such indicators as the number and quality of books written by members of the

2. See Tom Tanner and Eliza Smith Brown, "Why 100 ATS member schools have grown," ATS Commission on Accrediting (March 31, 2015); Tom Tanner, "Four Trends that may Portend the Future for ATS Enrollment," *Journal of Christian Ministry* (2017), 22–26; and "Seminary Enrollment Trends between 2008 and 2017," a chart of seminary comparisons published in 2017 by Dallas Theological Seminary. Copy in the GMR Papers housed at the seminary.

3. For a fuller development of this point see David F. Wells, *No Place for Truth* (1993), *God in the Wasteland* (1994), *Losing our Virtue* (1999), *Above all Earthly Powers* (2005) and *The Courage to be Protestant* (2017), all published by Eerdmans and *The Bleeding of the Evangelical Church* (Edinburgh: Banner of Truth, 1995).

faculty, the kinds of schools in which faculty members have studied or the number of notable faculty members who are teaching in their classrooms). As the surprisingly large number of applicants to Ivy League schools seems to indicate, students still want to attend those institutions that they believe can provide them with the highest quality education.

Shared Governance

A second area of concern has related to the understanding and practice of institutional governance. Final legal authority in freestanding seminaries like Gordon-Conwell, of course, rests entirely with the Board of Trustees.[4] Like most similar institutions, the Gordon-Conwell Board delegates day-to-day management responsibilities to the president whom they have selected, appointed and who serves at their pleasure.[5] Presidents, in their turn, characteristically delegate some of these responsibilities to administrative colleagues, such as an Academic Dean, who serve at their pleasure.

Since the publication in the 1966 of the *Statement on Government of Colleges and Universities*, issued jointly by the Association of Governing Boards of Universities and Colleges, the American Council on Education and the American Association of University Professors, however, the practice of "shared governance," as it

4. The seminary's bylaws state that the board of trustees has "sole governing authority over the seminary." Its "officers, namely, the chair, vice-chair, treasurer and secretary, are elected to serve for three years" but they are "not permitted to serve more than two consecutive terms in the same office." Under "the leadership of the chair, the board is responsible to review periodically the seminary's mission and educational programs, elect and review the president, and oversee the seminary's budget and endowment, salaries, tuition rates, and fees." See "Gordon-Conwell Theological Seminary 2015 Self Study Report to the Association of Theological Schools," published by the seminary, 2015, 101–4.

5. Gary A. Olson, "Exactly What is 'Shared Governance'?," *The Chronicle of Higher Education*, July 23, 2009, 1–5.

has come to be known, has emerged as the normative governance model within institutions of higher education.[6]

"Shared governance," as Steve Bahls has described it, is "a system for creating alignment" on "institutional direction" and "operational issues such as academic programs, tenure and promotion policies, budgeting, and student life" through the development of "common understandings of the challenges" facing the institution and "checks and balances" for the decisions that are reached. Although it often "takes a different form on every campus and at every institution," Bahls suggests, "it should align the faculty, board, and administration in common directions for decision-making regarding institutional direction, supported by a system of checks and balances for non-directional decisions."[7]

Both Gordon Divinity School and the Conwell School of Theology, of course, had been practicing their own versions of shared governance, or what might more accurately be called "collegial governance," long before the AAUPs "Statement on Government" was ever published.[8] Consequently, it seemed only natural that they would adopt such practices when the two institutions were merged in 1969. As the shared recollections of faculty members from that era amply attest, most of the seminary's official business seemed to take place informally and regularly at such occasions as the brown-bag lunch gatherings where colleagues from faculty and administration alike would meet for fellowship, gossip and discussion of campus issues. Long before any recommendations ever arrived on the formal agenda of the faculty or as a recommendation

6. American Association of University Professors, "Statement on Government of Colleges and Universities" (1966) and the Association of Governing Boards in Colleges and Universities, "Statement on Board Responsibility for Institutional Governance" (2010).

7. Steve Bahls, "What is Shared Governance?" the Association of Governing Boards of Universities and Colleges, AGB Blog, December 21, 2015, 1–2.

8. The more informal patterns of what might be called "collegial governance" often tended in practice to blur the important distinction between "shared governance" and "shared authority." Shared governance, while seeking to foster full participation by faculty, administration and board, insists that the final authority for decisions is the exclusive prerogative of the board and its administrative representatives.

to the Board of Trustees, colleagues had usually debated, argued, and reached consensus on virtually every detail of its provisions.

Equally significant, perhaps, is the fact that many members of the faculty during the 1970s and early 1980s also carried administrative responsibilities—directing admissions or registration or recruitment or participating in some other aspect of seminary leadership—so the traditional distinctions between faculty and administration were from the beginning characteristically blurred and indistinct. Even when the seminary's exploding growth made such distinctions necessary, it remained—at least, throughout the early decades of the institution's history—essentially a faculty-driven school. The Board of Trustee's final authority was fully recognized and respected, of course, but institutional decisions tended to be reached collegially and the board, with rare exception, accepted the recommendations placed before them by the faculty and administration. Fulltime administrators were few, trust within the seminary community was high and most disagreements tended to be resolved quickly and with relative ease.[9]

This culture of mutual trust and respect, in turn, enabled a strong, engaged and sometimes-feisty board to function comfortably with a strong, engaged and sometimes-feisty faculty. Furthermore, the powerful presence of the institution's two principal founders, Ockenga and Graham, seemed to provide a unique canopy under which the work of the seminary could move forward with only minimal disruptions. There were skirmishes from time to time, to be sure—when, for example, individual board members might take umbrage at the economic or political views of particular faculty members or when individual faculty members might take issue with positions espoused by members of the board—but few ever produced official actions by either body.[10] Academic deans,

9. During most of these early years, the seminary was administered by five full-time officers, each with one full-time secretary: a president, an executive vice president, an academic dean, a dean of students and a business manager.

10. Only when actions (whether by faculty or board) were taken by vote of the full body in formal session were they considered binding. Individual faculty and/or board members might express an opinion, as they often did, but such opinions had no binding power without formal action by the entire body.

for the most part, were expected to be advocates for faculty interests—from matters of curriculum to the selection of new faculty
colleagues—and presidents were expected to represent the policy
interests of the board. As one of the institution's strongest advocates for shared governance, President Robert E. Cooley continued
and deepened its practice when he was appointed as the seminary's
second president. This combination of shared governance, checks
and balances, loyalty to the institution, and a high level of collegial
trust enabled the young seminary to grow and flourish well into
the 1980s.

Since the full Board of Trustees normally gathered in formal
session on only three occasions each year, characteristically at
the beginning, middle, and close of each academic year, it saw fit
to authorize an Executive Committee (made up largely of board
members in the Boston area) to act on its behalf between formal
sessions.[11] It was this smaller body that was called upon during the
spring of 1985 to address a dispute that had broken out between
the faculty and the president. Representatives from the faculty, as
it happens, had written a letter to the president expressing their
concerns.[12]

Under normal circumstances, such an initiative might well
have resulted in the kinds of discussions and negotiations that had
for many years been part of the "checks and balances" tradition
of shared governance. When members of the Executive Committee learned about the letter, however, they decided to use the occasion to let the faculty know, in no uncertain terms, that such

11. The Executive Committee, upon recommendation of John Huffman
(Chairman of the Board from 2012 until 2018), was officially dissolved in
2010. Chairs of the Executive Committee throughout its history were Harold
Lindsell (1973–76), Allan Emery (1976–89), George Bennett (1989–99), Richard Armstrong (1999–2006) and Tom Colatosti (2006–10).

12. The letter was signed by most of the faculty members with continuing status (those without such status were not allowed to sign) and presented
in person to the president in early May of 1985 by Professors Roger Nicole,
Doug Stuart, and Carl Saylor. By mutual agreement, all drafts and copies of
the letter (with the exception of the single copy that was hand-delivered to
the president) were to be destroyed and the letter's contents were to remain
confidential. This writer has never seen a copy.

questioning of the president's authority would no longer be toler-ated.[13] Summoning all those who had signed the letter to gather at the Retreat House on Thursday, May 16th, 1985 they proceeded to call each one individually before the committee to communicate their displeasure.

The consequences were devastating. "Black Thursday," as it is still remembered, not only undermined overall faculty morale but it did serious damage to the seminary's historic tradition of collegial governance, decision-making, and its treasured culture of trust. Faculty members, having been thoroughly chastised, chose for the most part to quietly withdraw. There were exceptions, of course, but many simply disengaged—taking jobs in other institu-tions or limiting their on-campus activities to fulfilling their con-tractual obligations.

Although "Black Thursday's" long-term impact is more dif-ficult to assess, it is clear that it undermined the level of trust be-tween the faculty and the administration and it began to change the nature of governance at the seminary. The appointment of Sidney DeWaal as Vice President for Academic Affairs and Dean of the Seminary in 1988, a post he occupied until 1992, reflected in part a shift from the tradition of viewing the dean's office as rooted primarily in the faculty (serving as its primary voice and advocate) to one that was rooted primarily in administration (serving largely as a voice for the president and board).

The shift away from shared governance was further reflected in the appointment process for Kenneth Swetland to succeed Sidney DeWaal as Academic Dean in 1992.[14] When interviewed

13. The concern, at least for some trustees, tended to center on the issue of presidential authority. The longstanding tradition of "collegial governance," as practiced at the seminary, had blurred the line between "shared governance" and "shared authority." The Executive Committee saw the faculty letter as an opportunity to redraw the line between the two. As unintended consequences, however, the Executive Committee's handling of the matter also contributed to the gradual erosion of "shared governance," faculty participation in gover-nance and faculty ownership of institutional decisions.

14. When Dean Sidney DeWaal left the seminary to become President of what was then known as the Institute for Holy Land Studies (now the Jerusa-lem University College) in 1993, the three divisional chairs (Stuart, Rosell and

for the position by members of the board, only a single question was asked of him: "Ken, the board knows you, and we have only a single question to ask of you, namely 'Which direction is your chair facing?'" Taken somewhat aback by the question, Swetland responded with a smile, "Can I have a swivel chair?" When no smiles were returned and the committee simply answered, "No you can't," it was evident that the change from a largely faculty driven institution to a largely board and administration driven seminary had become a reality.[15]

Gradually, these changes began to transform the nature of governance at the seminary. Faculty meetings and retreats increasingly became occasions for reports from members of the administration rather than opportunities for robust faculty discussion and decision-making. Even traditional faculty prerogatives such as the management of the curriculum (namely, what is taught, when it is taught, who does the teaching and how it is taught) were increasingly transferred to administrators. "The responsibility of scheduling and delivery mode of courses," as President Hollinger reported to the faculty following the October 11, 2018 meeting of the Board of Trustees, has been moved by vote of the board "from faculty to the deans of each campus in consultation with the registrar and other appropriate personnel. This will ensure that student and campus needs are being fully met."[16]

Saylor) met with President Cooley to urge him to appoint Dr. Ken Swetland, a faculty colleague, to fill the post as Interim Dean. The following year, Dr. Swetland was formally appointed as Academic Dean, a post that he served with distinction for a decade.

15. Oral History Interview of Kenneth Swetland by Garth M. Rosell (November 9, 2012), GMR Papers housed at the seminary.

16. Dennis Hollinger, Institutional email Memo to the Gordon-Conwell Community, Tuesday, October 16, 2018. Copy in the GMR Papers housed at the seminary.

Hamilton Dean Ken Swetland and President Walt Kaiser[17]

Academic Freedom

Among the most difficult issues facing any seminary from time to time are those relating to theological orthodoxy. Since all members of the Gordon-Conwell faculty are required to sign the seminary's Statement of Faith annually, each is expected to conduct his/her research, writing, and teaching within its theological boundaries. When the work of a colleague is believed to have crossed those boundaries, as described in the *Faculty Handbook*, there is a clear process for testing whether such is actually the case. Central to this process, throughout the seminary's history, has been the Faculty Senate and its successor, the Faculty Personnel Policies

17. Dean Ken Swetland, who served under both Presidents Cooley and Kaiser, was succeeded (with several changes in official title) by Barry Corey, Frank James, Alice Mathews, Carol Kaminski, Rick Lints, Thomas Pfizenmaier, and Jeffrey Arthurs.

Committee. This faculty committee, chaired by the Vice President for Academic Affairs and whose seven faculty members their faculty colleagues elect annually, is charged with the responsibility of overseeing such cases and making recommendations for action, when needed, to the president and board.

The process has needed to be invoked only rarely. On each of those occasions, despite the high level of sensitivity and care with which the process is handled, the experience has proven to be both agonizing and painful for everyone involved. This was especially true, for example, following the publication in 1981 of Ramsey Michaels' book, *Servant and Son: Jesus in Parable and Gospel*. A long-time and much beloved teacher and colleague at Gordon-Conwell, Professor Michaels was eventually called before both the Faculty Personnel Policies Committee of the faculty and the Academic Affairs Committee of the Board of Trustees to respond to questions about whether parts of his book were consistent with the theological provisions in the contract to which he had signed his name.

Two basic questions were raised with respect to Professor Michaels' book: first, was his position consistent with the seminary's position on inerrancy as articulated in its Statement of Faith and second, was his view of the incarnation of Jesus consistent with the seminary's doctrinal affirmations? After a thorough and prayerful review by his peers, the Faculty Personnel Policies Committee determined that parts of the book were inconsistent with the seminary's theological position. Under the provisions of the *Faculty Handbook*, those conclusions would normally have led to the launching of formal proceedings against Professor Michaels. Before that occurred, however, Professor Michaels made the decision to resign his post and find employment elsewhere.

Although I was "assuming Jesus' pre-existence," Michaels later remarked,

> I made no secret of my use of literary and redaction criticism, and I discovered that the notion that Jesus had ever learned anything from anyone, even the Father, was profoundly disturbing to some. This came as a surprise, because such texts as Luke 2:20 and 52 and Hebrews 5:8

were well known and freely discussed among us. Perhaps the difficulty was that I envisioned the Father revealing himself to the Son in metaphor no less than in propositional discourse.

In any case, it became apparent that my days at Gordon-Conwell were numbered. Many students and some colleagues took my side, but the school was already polarized enough. I resigned in 1983, and was without a fulltime job for a year. Finally, twenty minutes before midnight on my fifty-third birthday, in a hotel in Tiberias by the Sea of Galilee, the overseas phone call came from Southwest Missouri State (now Missouri State) in Springfield, asking me to come for an interview. I took the job there in the fall of 1984 as Professor of Religious Studies.[18]

Although the debate over Professor Michaels' book eventually led to the loss of a respected colleague, it also reflected the institution's continuing commitment to its Basis of Faith and Statement of Mission. The courage displayed by members of the faculty, administration and trustees in their willingness to engage a difficult theological issue, to carefully apply due process to protect a colleague's interests and to arrive at a difficult consensus left some deep scars, to be sure, but it also reflected the seminary's determination to remain faithful to its theological and biblical foundations despite the great cost of doing so.

18. J. Ramsey Michaels, "Four Cords and an Anchor," in John Byron and Joel Lohr, eds., *I (Still) Believe: Biblical Scholars Share Their Stories on Faith and Scholarship* (Grand Rapids: Zondervan Academic, 2015), 173–85. Quotations are taken from pages 8 and 9. In his new Preface to *Servant and Son* (Eugene, OR: Wipf & Stock reprint, 2017), Professor Michaels remarks that the publication of *Servant and Son* "facilitated my resignation and departure from Gordon-Conwell Seminary in 1983" and that was "not altogether a bad thing, given that it ushered in eleven pleasant and productive years in the religious studies department at Southwest Missouri State (now Missouri State) University in Springfield. The issue was that my methodology and conclusions were judged to be inconsistent with the doctrine of biblical inerrancy, as defined by the seminary president, trustees, and faculty. Doubtless they were, and I had no interest by then in substituting my own definition just to keep a job. I had put in twenty-five good years at the seminary, and twenty-five was enough. I was ready for a change." The quotation is taken from page 1.

The seminary's New Testament Department Professors Gordon Fee, J.
Ramsey Michaels, David Scholer, and Andrew Lincoln

Institutional Mission and Identity

Perhaps the seminary's greatest challenge, throughout its first half
century, has been the continuing task of keeping the seminary's
founding vision (along with its statement of mission) fresh, robust,
and clearly in view. If the "main thing is to keep the main thing the
main thing," as Stephen Covey has cleverly suggested, then among
the seminary's most important responsibilities must certainly be
to ensure that every member of its community understands why
the seminary exists and wholeheartedly endorses the mission it
has promised to pursue. Such fidelity to founding principles is
exceedingly difficult to maintain and surprisingly rare. The more
normal pattern, it would seem, is the gradual drift from founding
principles and the eventual adoption of quite different missions
and identities.[19]

19. See for example George M. Marsden, *The Soul of the American*

New priorities, new goals and entirely new identities often replace the very priorities, goals and identities that brought the institutions into existence in the first place. Such changes can be as subtle and seemingly inconsequential as the decision to eliminate the old seminary bookcentre, to reduce the hours or services of the mailroom, or to change the dining room arrangements in the old cafeteria, places where students across the years have tended to gather to do business and to connect with one another. Yet such shifts, although sometimes necessary, can also have the unintended consequence of undermining the traditional seminary goal of developing community life and encouraging greater interaction between students and faculty.

More characteristic perhaps are the changes in priorities brought about by the inauguration of a new president, the appointment of a new faculty member, the arrival on campus of a new community of students, or a new addition to the board of trustees.

Sometimes these newer colleagues have simply reaffirmed old priorities, of course, as was the case in the appointment of President Kaiser, who brought fresh emphasis to the importance of preaching, or President White, who hoped to bring a renewed interest in the importance of the local church, or President Robinson, who helped the seminary to strengthen its Doctor of Ministry program, or President Hollinger, who focused greater attention on the importance of diversity.

University: From Protestant Establishment to Established Unbelief (New York: Oxford University Press, 1996) and Robert Benne, *Quality with Soul* (Grand Rapids: Eerdmans, 2001).

The Old Seminary Bookcentre

On other occasions, however, they have established new priorities and taken new initiatives that have laid their own claims on the seminary's limited budget. The expansion from one campus to four; the substantial growth in the size of the seminary administration; the adoption of new delivery systems for making the seminary's educational offerings available to students; the addition of new programs like those in leadership, Hispanic Studies, counseling, and spiritual formation; the construction of new student housing and the refurbishing of old spaces to accommodate the new programs have all added substance and sizzle to seminary life. They have also, however, made it increasingly difficult to provide the needed resources for what many consider to be the seminary's three most important priorities: namely, faculty, students, and the library. While the administration continues to grow, the faculty and student body continues to shrink.

The reshaping of priorities, while intended to bring benefits to the seminary, has also raised a far more difficult and vexing problem: namely, a growing uncertainty within the seminary about Gordon-Conwell's vision, identity and purpose. "Dear Colleagues," wrote the chair of the Division of Christian Thought in 2018, "I am hoping that you will be able to join us for an inter-divisional breakfast and discussion" on the "identity of 'Evangelicalism.'" Attached to this invitation was "a sketch for a proposed 'Global

Evangelicalism: 3.0.'"[20] For an evangelical seminary, founded by leaders like Harold John Ockenga and Billy Graham, such discussions are certainly nothing new. Within the contemporary cultural climate, however, they appear to reflect a growing *angst* among some within the seminary community as to who we are and why we are here. With the reality of declining enrollments and budget challenges on one hand and the demands of new priorities and initiatives on the other, many faculty members are engaging such discussions with a new kind of urgency.

The "genius" of the founders, some might argue with reference to these concerns, was their relentlessly *outward* orientation— their preoccupation with the proclamation of the gospel to every woman, man, boy, and girl on the planet, their commitment to the teaching and living out of sound doctrine in every arena of life and their determination to serve a desperately needy world with every ounce of energy at their disposal. The seminary's true identity and purpose, the founders were convinced, can only be found in Christ. We cannot hope to find it in ourselves, however diligent we are in self-analysis, nor can we discover it in either the cultural standards of our day, our evangelical identity or the intellectual fads that seek to please an itching ear. Indeed, there can be absolutely no question about who we are or why we are here,

20. "Inter-Divisional Breakfast," memo to members of the Hamilton faculty, March 3, 2018. Copy in the GMR Papers housed at the seminary.

our founders were convinced. The mission of Gordon-Conwell is not compelling because it is rooted in mid-twentieth-century evangelicalism. Rather, it is compelling because it flows directly from the Word of God.

"Let us ask ourselves," wrote Harold John Ockenga, "what is this organization accomplishing? Does it fit in with God's plan?" Is it "advancing God's cause?" God has planted us in this place and this time to fulfill what He has called us to do: namely, to do our utmost to encourage a "revival of Christianity in the midst of a secular world," to produce "scholars who can defend the faith on intellectual ground," to recapture "denominational leadership from within," to engage wholeheartedly in "reforms of the societal order," to provide "training and feeding of evangelical ministers into the churches," to establish "new evangelical seminaries" and fortify "existing evangelical seminaries with additional professors and funds," to train students who will graduate "with a certainty and knowledge expressed by 'Thus saith the Lord' and with a practical program joined with passion."[21]

In the midst of a noisy and fragmented world, marked by competing interests, selfish demands, difficult challenges, and siren voices, our founders seem to be pleading with us to keep "the main thing the main thing"—namely, the godly, rigorous, and Bible-centered training of men and women who, empowered by the Holy Spirit, will "expect great things from God" and "attempt great things for God."[22]

---

21. Harold John Ockenga, "Resurgent Evangelical Leadership," *Christianity Today* (October 10, 1960), 11–15.

22. Quotation is attributed variously to the missionary statesmen, Adoniram Judson and William Carey.

CHAPTER XI

From Kaiser to Hollinger

Students want to study with faculty members who are renowned for
having achieved in their fields of study and service and that is what
they will get at Gordon-Conwell

—WALTER C. KAISER JR.

AT HIS INSTALLATION AS the seminary's third president, Walter C.
Kaiser, Jr. promised his listeners that he would "invest one hundred percent" of his "time and energies into leading this institution
under God to as great heights as any of us could yet have imagined
or dreamed possible as we enter the twenty-first century." Given
the enormous "forces and movements that are already at work
globally," he conjectured, you are probably wondering if this is too
lofty a goal for a new president to set, too hard a task for us to un-
dertake, too "raging a fire" to quench with a "squirt gun or a water-
pistol." Indeed, the challenge may appear so daunting, in fact, "that
it may seem more reasonable to quietly surrender with a saner
reallocation of the lives of our sons and daughters, our intellectual
powers, and our financial resources to something that had much

better odds of succeeding." However, he quickly added, would this not be an admission that some things are too hard for God?[1]

Such acquiescence, the new president was convinced, would be neither wise nor prudent. For God has provided us with all the tools necessary to fulfill his purposes for us. "Just what tools, emphases, or methods, you ask, would I propose that a seminary, much less an evangelical seminary, employ in the twenty-first century that could in any stretch of the imagination be of any usefulness in tempering the powerful gains of a secular society with its accompanying denials of Isaiah's majestic Lord?" "First and foremost," he suggested, it will take "persons who have experienced the unique call of God to be individuals who can stand in the spiritual, ethical and ontological gap that our times have created." Like "'a burning fire shut up' in the inner being," this call from God "overrules every difficulty" and "takes joy in all kinds of sacrifices for the sake of the work itself." The "real shakers and movers of the twenty-first century" will be those "women and men who are willing to give themselves to the rigors of spiritual formation along with the rigors of intellectual investment in all that is taught and researched in the academy."

A second component must be the "older teachers and mentors" that will serve as their models and guides. The "new evangelical seminary of the twenty-first century must emphasize 'high touch,'" that is, "mentoring relationships" with a faculty ready and willing to share "their lives with the students so that a holistic development of the whole person might be part and parcel of the educational experience." Consequently, he continued, we will seek to strengthen the faculty "even further by a most aggressive system of recruiting the best equipped faculty that we can find on planet earth. Students want to study with faculty members who are renowned for having achieved in their fields of study and service— and that is what they will get at Gordon-Conwell." Our faculty, therefore, will "be women and men whose lives and characters

---

1. Quotations are taken from Walter C. Kaiser, Jr., "The Evangelical Seminary of the Twenty-First Century," in *Hilltop*, Vol. 9, No. 2 (Fall 1997), 1 and 11.

radiate their confidence in an incomparably great God who is sovereign over their lives in every detail, including their minds. They shall be possessed of a burning desire to see Christ's Church prosper and the evangelistic mandate of the Savior supply their mission and purpose for all their work, both individually and as a team—after all, a seminary is a handmaiden to the Church and not a unit to itself or one related in the first place to the university. But for all of this, they shall nonetheless be unafraid to investigate every nook and cranny of truth wherever it is found, for their understanding is that all truth, no matter where it is found or who said it, is still God's truth and exists because of the One who upholds all things simply by a word." Consequently, our faculty will "excel as communicators in the classroom, as researchers in the study, and as writers who interact and publish in the marketplace of the academy and plazas of the populace. They shall exhibit the academic freedom of the academy, but not a freedom without limit, or without limits even to God. Instead, their freedom in Christ has made them freest of all persons to follow all truth wherever its leads, for it will be anchored in a proper awareness of each mortal's limitations, especially the inhibiting bondage of sin in any claims to complete and total autonomy." With students who are called by God and a well-trained and spiritually-mature faculty, President Kaiser was convinced, Gordon-Conwell Theological Seminary will be able to fulfill its mission" and serve Christ's church around the world. For God is "still calling out the best minds of our day to dedicate their lives to serving him body, soul and mind to the glory of His great name." [2]

President Kaiser's inaugural address became, in a sense, a kind of template for his presidency. With the assistance of his Academic Dean, Ken Swetland, three gifted scholars were soon added to the faculty: Duane Garrett in Old Testament, Gary A. Parrett in Christian Education and Timothy C. Tennent in World Missions.[3] With the help of Barry H. Corey, the seminary's Vice President for

2. Quotations are taken from Walter C. Kaiser, Jr., "The Evangelical Seminary of the Twenty-First Century," *Hilltop*, Vol. 9, No. 2 (Fall 1997), 1 and 11.

3. "Seminary Welcomes Three New Professors," *Hilltop*, Vol. 10, No. 1 (Summer 1998), 1.

Development, a new student scholarship program was launched and "plans were laid for a major fundraising campaign to support a number of new initiatives proposed by this administration and the leadership team."[4] With the assistance of Eldin Villafane, Executive Director of the Contextualized Urban Theological Education Enablement Program (CUTEEP), a major urban theological education conference was planned for Boston.[5] And during the 1997–98 "Inaugural Year" several distinguished speakers were brought to campus, a Summer Language Institute was planned, a faculty New England Spiritual Heritage Tour was conducted, three new Doctor of Ministry tracks were introduced and a new Academic Dean, David Wells, was appointed for the Charlotte campus.[6]

Professor Gwenfair Adams Speaking to the Faculty in Northampton

Expanding into Jacksonville

Among President Kaiser's initiatives was the decision to expand the seminary from three campus settings to four. "Beginning in February of 2006," announced a seminary news article in *Contact* magazine, "students will be able to take Gordon-Conwell classes in

4. "Campaign Discussions Underway," *Hilltop*, Vol. 9, No. 1 (Fall 1997), 9.

5. "Agenda for a New Millennium," *Hilltop*, Vol. 9, No. 1 (Fall 1997), 8.

6. See the *Hilltop*, Vol. 9, No. 1 (Fall 1997) and Vol. 10, No. 1 (Summer 1998).

Jacksonville, Florida. Through the impetus of a group of Jacksonville alumni/ae pastors and other church leaders led by Dr. Robert Morris, pastor of First Presbyterian Church, a new extension site of the Charlotte campus is being established in that community. The church leaders approached the seminary some years ago about providing courses in their region and have subsequently raised substantial funds and pledges to operate the new extension site. Trustees approved the project at the May Board meeting."[7]

Having observed the development of the Charlotte campus and aware that no seminary had yet been established in northeastern Florida, President Kaiser asked the Academic Dean at Charlotte, Dr. Sidney Bradley, to explore the possibility further. Consequently, Dean Bradley—without whose considerable administrative skills the Jacksonville campus would not exist—took up the task with his characteristic competence and quiet determination. After appointing Kent Gilbert to oversee the project, planning began in earnest. The results were encouraging both in terms of community support and student interest. On Friday evening, February 9, 2006, twenty-seven students gathered at 5:30 p.m. in a room provided by the First Presbyterian Church to begin Jacksonville's very first class.[8] "We are excited about expanding our program to Florida," Dean Bradley remarked, and "we look forward to working closely with them to develop a strong accredited program of theological education for their region."[9]

Within ten years of its founding, student enrollment at Jacksonville had grown to nearly one hundred.[10] "Our local board of advisors has been instrumental to our growth, meeting frequently with the Jacksonville staff and introducing them to friends who

7. "Gordon-Conwell to Open Jacksonville Extension in 2006," *Contact*, Vol. 35, No. 1 (Summer 2005), 36.

8. The course was "Church History from the Reformation" taught by Professor Rosell.

9. *Contact*, Vol. 35, No. 1 (Summer 2005), 36. See also "Gordon-Conwell Theological Seminary Five Year Financial Plan, Jacksonville Extension Site," a six page document (April 21, 2004) in the GMR Papers housed at the seminary.

10. "Jacksonville Campus: A Year of Growth," *Annual Report 2017: For the Glory of God*, an annual publication by the seminary, 9.

have an affinity with Gordon-Conwell," remarked Ryan Reeves, Associate Professor of Historical Theology and Jacksonville's former Assistant Dean.

Taken together, the "Kaiser Years" (from 1997 to 2006) were marked by significant numerical growth throughout the seminary—expanding Gordon-Conwell's combined student population from more than 900 to 2,212 students drawn "from 44 nations" and making Gordon-Conwell "the 5th largest seminary in North America." The faculty, moreover, was also increased by the addition of "thirty new professors" and "scholarship funding" for students was "increased by more than 300 percent."

Bob Landrebe, Executive VP and Chief Financial Officer[11]

11. Bob Landrebe, who served for many years with grace and exceptional skill as Executive Vice President and Chief Financial Officer during the seminary's years of largest growth and expansion, was preceded in that office by Clayton Sidell and Glenn Beernink and followed by Jay Trewern who since 2012 has overseen this area as the Vice President for Finance and Operations and Chief Financial Officer.

With respect to the maintenance and development of facilities, campus buildings in Charlotte, Boston and Hamilton were all either updated or retrofitted (including the Phippen, Gray and Lamont Halls in the Kerr Building) and renovations or additions were made to the Great Room, the Student Center, the Dining Commons, the Goddard Library, the Student Life offices, the Kerr Building patio and the Wilson House. In addition, as reported in *Contact* magazine, students on all four campuses were benefitting from numerous new academic and spiritual life programs, such as the Center for Preaching, the Pierce Center for Disciple-Building, Compass for high school youth, the J. Christy Wilson, Jr. Center for World Missions, the Center for the Study of Global Christianity, Semlink distance learning now available in Chinese, and free Dimensions of the Faith courses used by churches and missionaries across the globe." Financial undergirding for many of these initiatives was provided by President Kaiser's successful $54 million capital campaign.[12]

---

12. These figures were reported in "Honoring Our Third President," *Contact* magazine, Vol. 36, No. 1 (Winter 2007), 30–31.

President Walt Kaiser and Academic Dean Barry Corey

What most marked the Kaiser years, however, was the sheer sense of joy that President Kaiser seemed to find in the work he was doing. "My nine years as President," Walt remarked to the more than four hundred who had gathered for his retirement dinner, were "by all odds the best years of my life. They were the happiest years. There was a lot of work, but it was fun work and it was fun all the way through." Indeed, the "sheer joy of working with people who really had a mind to work together and wanted to see things accomplished for the Lord" is what we will remember and cherish the most.[13]

13. Interview with President Kaiser, "The best years of my life: Reflections

The combined thirty-seven-year tenures of the seminary's first three presidents—Ockenga, Cooley, and Kaiser—comprise an overwhelming percentage of the institution's history. Their task, at least in one sense, had been to manage a continually growing community of faculty and students. Having begun in 1969 with 279 students a single campus, Gordon-Conwell Theological Seminary had by 2006 reached the largest enrollment it would ever achieve throughout its first half-century of existence—expanding to an incredible 2,212 women and men studying on four campus settings.[14] By the grace of God, the seminary had become one of the largest theological training centers in all of North America.

on Nine Years as President," *Contact* magazine, Vol. 36, No. 1 (Winter 2007), 31–32.

14. "Gordon-Conwell Theological Seminary at a Glance (Fall 2006) published by the seminary's registration office and based on numbers from the ATS Enrollment Reports for Fall 2006.

As John Fletcher had warned, however, such striking growth would over time prove to be exceedingly difficult to maintain.[15] Indeed, there is a sense in which the seminary's next three presidents—White, Robinson, and Hollinger—inherited a very different set of tasks than those faced by their three predecessors given the fact that an overall student population that had peaked in 2006 with 2,212 students had gradually declined to 1,646 students by the Fall Semester of 2018. In a largely tuition-driven institution, of course, the loss of more than five hundred students over a relatively short period of time can place enormous strains on an institutional budget.

Adding to the difficulties moreover, especially during the seminary's fifth decade, was the enormous loss of tuition revenue when the old Semlink program was replaced in 2014 by the new Semlink+ program.[16] Between 2006 and 2018, moreover, two of the seminary's four campuses experienced sharp declines in the number of enrolled students.[17]

15. John C. Fletcher, *The Futures of Protestant Seminaries* (Washington, DC: The Alban Institute, 1983), 27–59.

16. According to statistics supplied by the seminary's registration office, the number of students enrolled in "Classic Semlink" courses in 2008 was 1,105 (who were enrolled that year for a total of 1,799 courses). The total number of students enrolled for Semlink+ courses in 2016 was reported to be 218.

17. Detailed enrollment figures during these years can be found in the comparative report (covering the years between 2006 and 2018) produced by the Registration Office for discussion by the faculty at one of its regular meetings in the Fall of 2018 and updated in "At a Glance: 2018–2019 Enrollment and Graduation Statistics" published in 12/11/2018. Copies can be found in the GMR Papers housed at the seminary.

The Great Room on the Hamilton Campus

The Hollinger Years

Given the relatively brief presidencies of Jim White and Haddon Robinson, the primary task of responding to these challenges fell on the shoulders of the seminary's sixth president, Dennis Hollinger.[18] With a background in both the academy and the church, President Hollinger was well aware that new sources of funding would be needed to ensure a strong and vibrant future for the seminary.

18. Dennis Hollinger was installed as the seminary's sixth president and Professor of Christian Ethics on August 1, 2008, succeeding Haddon W. Robinson, its fifth president, who served in that capacity from May of 2007 until August of 2008. Its fourth president, James Emery White, served as president from October 6, 2006 until May of 2007. See *Contact* magazine, "Inaugurating Gordon-Conwell's Fourth President," Vol. 36, No. 1 (Winter 2007) and *Contact* magazine, "Gordon-Conwell's New President," Vol. 37, No. 1 (Summer 2008), 3–7.

Rick Lints (Provost) and Dennis Hollinger (President)

Consequently, with the approval and support of the Board of Trustees and the assistance of the Campaign Steering Committee, President Hollinger helped to launch in 2010 a comprehensive, six-year campaign to raise in excess of sixty-eight million dollars for the various needs of the seminary.[19] "Our Legacy—Our Future, Serving the Church with Excellence and Innovation," as the campaign was called, officially ended on June 30, 2016, having raised nearly 70 million dollars—"the largest successful campaign in the history of the seminary," as John Huffman, Chair of the Board of Trustees, was able to report, "raising nearly $30 million (in current cash and future planned gifts) and funding 32 new scholarship funds" in addition to providing "sufficient funds to upgrade fifty aging, on-campus Hamilton apartments" and "donations to complete and dedicate the David M. Rogers Hall of Missions at the Charlotte Campus."[20]

19. For the membership of the Campaign Steering Committee see "Reflections from the President," in *For the Glory of God: Campaign Edition, Annual Report 2016*, 5–7.

20. John Huffman, "Our Legacy—Our Future," in *For the Glory of God: Campaign Edition, Annual Report 2016*, 3–4.

"Basically, I've done three things in my life:" remarked President Hollinger soon after arriving on campus, "the pastorate for 11 years, full-time seminary professor for 11 years, and educational leadership for the last 11 years. My sense was that this background was very much along the lines of what Gordon-Conwell wanted and needed." I have also, he continued, "felt a real pull to Gordon-Conwell because of the unique delivery systems of each campus. Because I was an urban pastor, the CUME program resonates with us. The adult education model of the Charlotte campus is very timely and appealing. Simultaneously, I'm at heart very much a classicist when it comes to education, and that's very much a part of the Hamilton campus. The varied models of the three campuses certainly played a role in being a good fit with our own passions for theological education. And I have deep respect for the history of Gordon-Conwell, particularly the significant role it has played in New England evangelicalism." With respect to a question about his own passions and commitments, he remarked, the "concept of holding things in balance has been central to my commitments over the years, in the life of pastoring, teaching and administration." And as a seminary student in the 1970s, he became (as he phrased it) deeply engaged with "the whole issue of social responsibility" and the important questions relating to "how we live out our evangelical faith in the midst of culture and society."[21]

Recognizing that such a capital campaign needed to be coupled with a thorough review of campus priorities and policies, President Hollinger and his administrative team linked the "Our Legacy—Our Future" capital campaign with the preparation of a long-range strategic plan. Five strategic goals were established with the strong support of the Board of Trustees: namely, the creation "of a more robust and integrated educational experience" for students; the engagement with greater intentionality "in the globalization of the church"; the expansion of "student access" to theological education "through multiple delivery systems"; the establishment of "a culture of outcomes and assessment"; and the improvement of "the

21. Interview with "Gordon-Conwell's New President," *Contact* magazine, Vol. 37, No. 1 (Summer 2008), 3–7.

seminary's financial strength"; and "five key initiatives and action steps for achieving the goals" were identified: namely, to "reach out to underserved student markets; to "establish new global partnerships"; to "optimize our existing educational program"; to "implement curricular review"; and to ensure an adequate resourcing for the initiatives. Among the most significant implementation efforts flowing from the strategic plan were the establishment in 2009 of the Hispanic Ministries Program, an effort by the seminary to "provide top-quality theological education to Hispanics"; the launching of the BibleJourney-Biblical Literacy Project, under the guidance of the Robert C. Cooley Center in Charlotte, to make instruction in the Bible more widely accessible; and the establishment of several important new global partnerships.[22]

Jacksonville Graduate Isidro Mangual Salas with Professor Ryan Reeves[23]

22. Quotations taken from the *Gordon-Conwell Theological Seminary 2015 Self Study Report to the Association of Theological Schools*, a 129-page report prepared in advance of the 2015 accreditation visit by ATS and NEASC, 12–25. Copy available in Goddard Library on the Hamilton campus.

23. *Annual Report 2017: For the Glory of God*, published by the seminary, photo taken from page 9.

Despite these efforts, however, it soon became apparent that further measures would be needed to address the financial short-falls that began to arrive with increasing frequency. Consequently, the Board of Trustees appointed a Task Force to explore ways and means by which the financial shortfalls might be remedied. After much discussion and prayer, the Task Force presented its report and recommendations to the full board for its consideration. At a 2016 meeting of the Board of Trustees, what came to be called the "nine initiatives" were discussed and adopted unanimously in an effort, as reported in an announcement from the President's Office, to "enable Gordon Conwell to efficiently, and with excellence, ful-fill its vision and mission by ensuring good fiscal stewardship." The goal of these initiatives, also noted in the announcement, was "to annually net operational benefits totaling $1,000,000" by the close of the 2017–18 fiscal year so as "to address compensation increases while still working with a balanced budget."[24]

Faculty/Student Lobster Bake in 2007

24. Gordon-Conwell Theological Seminary, "Stewarding the Future of Gordon-Conwell—Nine Initiatives," a two-page document published by the President's Office. Copy available in the GMR Papers housed at the seminary.

Word of the nine initiatives spread quickly throughout the seminary community. Some supported the changes, seeing them as perhaps unfortunate but necessary. Others were troubled by some of its provisions and directives, most especially those relating to the dismissal of the Ockenga Institute's beloved and longtime director, David Horn, the proposed changes in cafeteria service (fearing its potential damage to the building of "community" on campus) and the systematic reorganization of the Ockenga Institute itself. Others worried that key ministries of the institute, the synergistic organization that since 1985 had provided such a vital bridge between the seminary and the church, would be diminished or lost in the process. While it is certainly true that the nine initiatives were able to bring a measure of financial relief to the seminary budget, their benefits had come at considerable cost.

Despite the seminary's continuing budgetary challenges, however, much of its educational work continued to enjoy the blessings of God.[25] Hundreds of students, including many remarkable young men and women like Claudia Nahmias Melo Carvalho da Silva, a Brazilian obstetrician and gynecologist who was a student on our Charlotte campus before she and her husband Eduardo followed God's call as medical missionaries, continued to enroll on one or another of the seminary's four campuses.[26] Dozens of dedicated and well-trained faculty members continued to teach their large introductory lecture classes and small intensive seminar courses to the eager students who made their way into their

25. As the seminary's former Vice President for Advancement, Kurt W. Drescher, remarked in 2017, "I think a lot about seminary education as we look at the changing landscapes of seminaries across the country. When we hear of institutions like ours struggling with enrollment challenges, it sometimes feels a bit like a test in patience and perseverance: Can we stand the test of time? However, when I feel like that, our great God seems always to provide an encouraging, heartwarming and even profound reminder of why we do what we do." See Kurt W. Drescher, "Why Do We Do What We Do?" in *Annual Report 2017: For the Glory of God*, 12–13.

26. For the inspiring story of Claudia and her husband Eduardo, see Anne B. Doll, "A Missionary Who Happens to be a Doctor," in Gordon-Conwell Theological Seminary *Annual Report 2017, For the Glory of God*, published by the seminary, 4–5.

classrooms.[27] Opportunities for students to study abroad, including exciting new courses such as Todd Johnson's travel seminar to "Silk Road" sites, were provided under the leadership of Mary Ann Hollinger. Dozens of luncheon forums and workshops, featuring speakers from around the world, enhanced the seminary's regular curriculum. Unique worship experiences, as part of the chapel programs on our several campuses, provided opportunities for personal and corporate devotion to God. Special musical events, such as the opportunity to hear the world-famous Boston Symphony Orchestra, were scheduled by faculty members like Ed Keazirian and made possible by former students such as Elisabeth Ostling, an artist with the BSO orchestra. And hundreds of bright, dedicated and well-prepared graduates joined the seminary's more than ten thousand alumni/ae in serving God as pastors, missionaries, teachers, lawyers, public servants, counselors, and in dozens of additional callings.

"Gordon-Conwell Theological Seminary has long been known as a place of academic rigor," President Hollinger remarked in 2017. "When Harold John Ockenga, Billy Graham and J. Howard Pew brought together two schools to form a new seminary in 1969, they emphasized the need for an institution that would love God with the mind. This meant in-depth knowledge of God's Word, utilizing the original languages, enabling students to think theologically with depth, and grappling honestly with pressing intellectual and cultural/social questions of the day. That academic rigor has remained over the years, and the questions and issues have not gotten any easier."[28]

27. Among the recently appointed faculty members were Pam Davis, Associate Professor of Counseling and Director of the Counseling Department at the Charlotte campus; Seong Hyun Park, Dean of the Boston campus; Virginia Ward, Assistant Professor of Youth and Leadership Development and Assistant Dean at the Boston campus; Nicole Martin, Assistant Professor of Ministry and Leadership Development at the Charlotte campus; Jacqueline Dyer, Assistant Professor of Counseling at the Boston campus; Jason Hood, Assistant Professor of New Testament and Director of Advanced Urban Ministerial Education at the Boston campus; and Deana Nail, Dean of Students and Director of the Master of Divinity degree program on the Charlotte campus.

28. Quotation from Dennis Hollinger, "President's Report," in *Annual*

"In recent years," Hollinger continued, "we have come to see that along with academic excellence, we must also engender spiritual development in the lives of our students. Good education requires a depth of learning, but theological education for ministry also entails a formation of personal discipleship." We believe, President Hollinger concluded, that "at Gordon-Conwell we have the unique opportunity of bringing together academic rigor with spiritual formation. Schools tend to emphasize one or the other, but we believe it's possible to simultaneously pursue both."[29]

Drawing upon seminary resources such as the Pierce Center, the Ockenga Institute, the Doctor of Ministry offerings and a variety of additional programs on each of our campuses, the seminary has increasingly embraced the need to shift its efforts, as Provost Lints expressed it, "from informational to formational, from being a professional school to a school of discipleship." Such an emphasis is nothing new, he continued, but rather "one that has constantly pressed in on the life of seminaries. The unique moment we live in has made these evolutionary changes more pronounced in our relationship to the culture and the present needs of the Church. Our mandate," Lints concluded, "is to prepare healthy pastors and leaders who can speak and live faithfully, no longer taking for granted that the mediating structures of our culture naturally reinforce a vital Christian faith."[30]

Report 2017: For the Glory of God (So. Hamilton, MA: by the seminary, 2017), 3.

29. Continuing quotations are taken from Hollinger, "President's Report," 2017, 3.

30. Quotations are taken from Provost Richard Lints as quoted in "Hamilton Campus: A Year of Transitions," *Annual Report 2017: For the Glory of God*, Gordon-Conwell Theological Seminary, 2017, 6.

CHAPTER XII

Future Prospects

The future is as bright as the promises of God

—WILLIAM CAREY

"THE MAIN THING," AS Stephen Covey reminds us, "is to keep the main thing the main thing."[1] Since the years of its founding, as we have discovered, Gordon-Conwell Theological Seminary has been guided by the clear vision of its founders, by its deep commitment to historic biblical Christianity, by the theological formulations of its statement of faith and by the six articles of its statement of mission. Although the siren voices of financial expediency, cultural accommodation and the easing of standards continue to make their case throughout higher education, Gordon-Conwell has remained committed, in the words of its mission, to the task of maintaining "academic excellence in the highest tradition of Christian scholarship in the teaching of the biblical, historical and theological disciplines." When the "winds of change blow across the landscape of theological education," as the seminary's second president reflected in 1993, "we do not strive to be all things to all people."

1. Stephen R. Covey, *The 8th Habit: From Effectiveness to Greatness* (New York: Free Press, 2005), 160.

185

Rather, "we do strive to be responsive to the needs of God's world within the context of our mission. Here at Gordon-Conwell we remain a center of classical theological education. This is a place where students may come to live, learn, and distill the traditional teachings of a scholarly community. This is a place where students may come to be spiritually formed. Here, our common endeavor is to understand God." [2]

Seminary Faculty Based in Hamilton (2018) [3]

Having just returned to the United States after a breakthrough preaching mission in the Soviet Union, Billy Graham—in a stirring 1982 commencement address—reminded the seminary

2. Robert E. Cooley, "President's Message," *Gordon-Conwell Theological Seminary Catalog 1993–1994*, published by the seminary, 2.

3. Photo of the Seminary Faculty based in Hamilton by Nicole Rim (used by permission). From left to right: Gwenfair Adams, Gordon Isaac, Matthew Kim, Adonis Vidu, Jeffrey Arthurs, Todd Johnson, Pablo Polischuk, Mateus de Campos, Xiyi Yao, Rick Lints (VP Academic), Kateryna Kuzubova, David Currie, Dennis Hollinger (President), Jim Singleton, Thomas Pfizenmaier (Academic Dean), Sean McDonough, Emmett Price, Doug Stuart, Jack Davis, Ken Barnes, Karen Mason, Tom Petter, Jeff Niehaus, Donna Petter, and Carol Kaminski.

graduates of the dangerous, challenging and often costly claim that God has made on their lives and on their seminary. Using the story of a remarkable young missionary as his point of reference, he warned the graduates that they may be called upon to face suffering and persecution in fulfilling their callings. "To serve [God] is costly," he remarked, "but the reward is overwhelming in this life and the life to come." It is my prayer for each of you that "your determination when you leave here" will be to fulfill your callings "with no reserve, no retreat and no regrets."[4]

Billy Graham Speaking at 1994 Commencement

By God's grace, there is reason to believe that the vital work of Gordon-Conwell Theological Seminary—begun with such urgency and clarity of purpose by our godly founders half a century ago—will continue to flourish for many years to come. None should dare to presume that the blessing of God forever remains upon any human institution. The "Ichabods" of history provide ample evidence of the folly of such a presumption. Nonetheless,

4. William F. Graham, "No Reserve, No Retreat, No Regrets," 1982 Commencement Address at Gordon-Conwell Theological Seminary, reprinted in *Contact* magazine, Vol. 12, No. 2 (Commencement 1982), 17–19. The young missionary was William Whiting Borden. For his story see Mrs. Howard Taylor, *Borden of Yale '09, "The Life that Counts"* (Philadelphia and Toronto: China Inland Mission, 1926).

as the seminary begins its second half-century there is cause for genuine hope for intellectual and spiritual renewal.

In times of great need—throughout the history of this seminary and in the stories of other Christian organizations—God has been faithful in providing godly, visionary, and well-trained leaders to help point the way, reset the priorities and restore the vision. On the eve of its fiftieth anniversary, Gordon-Conwell Theological Seminary has yet again, by God's grace, been given such an opportunity with the appointment of Dr. Scott Sunquist as its seventh president. A "missionary, scholar, pastor, and administrator," as Bishop Claude Alexander has characterized the new president-elect, Dr. Sunquist will help to enable the seminary to "raise up new leaders with a passion for reaching the world for Christ. He is a transformative leader who can usher Gordon-Conwell into its brightest years."[5]

5. Bishop Claude Alexander, the Chairman of the Board of Trustees, "Gordon-Conwell Names New President-Elect Dr. Scott Sunquist," in an announcement to the seminary community, Friday, October 12, 2018. See also "Board of Trustees Names Missiologist to Lead Gordon-Conwell," Annual Report 2018: For the Glory of God (South Hamilton: by the Seminary, 2019), 5. Copies in the GMR Papers housed at the seminary. The seminary's sixth president, Dennis Hollinger, will officially retire at the end of the 2018–2019 academic year. He has served in that office since June 2008.

Dr. Scott Sunquist, the Seminary's 7th President

The challenges facing President Sunquist are formidable. Externally, the rapidly changing cultural trends, rising costs, demographic shifts, the role of technology, town/gown relations, accreditation standards, partnership with the church, and a host of additional challenges await his attention. Internally, important issues such as student enrollment, faculty appointments, salaries and benefits, theological boundaries, the proper role of distance education, sibling rivalries between campuses, and a host of other challenges will face the new president. Most pressing of all, some would contend, is the need for the seminary to be "mission driven" in everything it does! While good management is always needed, a robust and joyful faithfulness to God's mission—expressed in the vision voiced so powerfully by our institution's founders and reflected so clearly in the seminary's magnificent Statement of Mission—is essential.

"What kind of a future do we face?" asked Billy Graham when he addressed the graduating class of 1994. "We seem to be entering a new age," Graham told the students, one that is marked by "ethnic and racial strife," "social upheaval," "collapsing moral standards," "growing hostility to God's truth," "upheaval in the Church" and "secularization of the Christian faith." Yet despite these problems, he added, I believe that "this is the greatest moment to be in the ministry of the Lord that there has ever been in the history of the Christian church"—since with his commission, God has promised us nothing less than his presence and guidance.[6] "The early apostles carried the flaming truths of the Gospel far and wide," Graham reminded his listeners, "they scattered" and "surmounted obstacles" and "overcame difficulties" and "endured persecution." These "men and women of the past have handed a torch to us" and "we must dare to believe God for even greater things in the years to come."[7]

Theological education, in short, is serious business—and it is serious precisely because it is undertaken (by students, teachers, trustees, supporters and administrators alike) in the very Name of God and in the service of God's mission to a needy world. The founders of Gordon-Conwell Theological Seminary, who carried the torch for so many years with such courage and grace, have passed it to us with their blessing and with their full expectation that, by God's grace, each succeeding generation will carry it faithfully and joyfully until the return of the risen Christ!

6. Billy Graham, "Preaching with Boldness in a World of Upheaval," published in the *Contact* magazine, Vol. 23, No. 2 (Fall 1994), 3–9, quotations from page 4.

7. Graham, "No Reserve, No Retreat, No Regrets," 17.

Afterword

Writing a book is an adventure. To begin with, it is a toy and an
amusement; then it becomes a mistress, and then it becomes a
master, and then a tyrant.

—WINSTON CHURCHILL

BY ITS VERY NATURE, I had heard, the writing of an institutional
history inevitably becomes a community project. The truth of this
old adage began to dawn on me when I sent a copy of an early
faculty photo to several colleagues asking for their help in identifying its date, provenance, and the names of the faculty members
whose images I could not identify. To my astonishment, these
friends picked up the project immediately and they began to invite
a goodly number of others to join them in the search. Soon a rapidly growing and interconnected stream of emails began arriving
on my computer as gifted sleuths like Meirwyn and Nina Walters,
Robin and Jack Davis, Mark and Paula Nickels, Ken Swetland,
Doug Stuart, and others looked for clues and interacted with each
other's findings. As a result, not only were the date and provenance
of the photo confirmed with reasonable certainty but all (except-
ing one) of the faculty members in the picture were clearly identified. The discovery that colleagues, with busy schedules of their
own, would respond to my request with such alacrity and zest was

a nice reminder that the story I have tried to tell is not so much mine as theirs.

The truth of the old adage came in other ways as well. The thirty-four individuals who filled nearly one hundred "oral history" tapes with their reflections, remembrances, and insights also underscored for me the communal ownership of Gordon-Conwell Theological Seminary's history. Special thanks are due to those who so readily and enthusiastically participated in these interviews. Included in this remarkable group of friends and colleagues are John Huffman, Doug Stuart, Rick Lints, Dennis Hollinger, Scott Gibson, Richard Gross, Ken Umenhofer, Tim Laniak, Ray Pendleton, Jack Davis, Dave Horn, Doug and July Hall, David Wells, Lurline (Mears) Umenhofer, Leighton Ford, Carl and Avis Saylor, Lita Schlueter, Haddon Robinson, Tim Tennent, Ed Keazirian, Patricia Nielsen, James Emery White, Bob Cooley, Ryan Reeves, Eldin Villafane, Ken Swetland, Sid Bradley, and representatives from our outstanding seminary staff.[1]

Special thanks are also in order for the seminary's outstanding library staff, including the Head Librarian, Robert Mayer and his colleagues Meredith Kline, Jim Darlack, Robert McFadden, Matt Wasielewski and others, who without exception responded with grace and timeliness to my numerous requests. The seminary's amazing archival holdings, including boxes 19–31 (relating to the institution's history) in the Harold John Ockenga Papers, were of enormous help in my research. Materials from my own books and papers that are referenced in the footnotes, including a variety of documents, oral history interviews, minutes, letters, and other materials collected over thirty-seven years at the seminary, have been donated to the seminary and will become part of the seminary's collection in 2020. The papers will be housed on the Charlotte campus and the books in the Rosell Seminar Room on the Hamilton campus.

---

1. The "Oral History Project," conducted between 2012 and 2018, was part of the research for this book. The taped interviews are now part of the GMR Papers housed at the seminary.

Thanks are also due to Nicole Rim for her assistance with institutional photos; to Anne Doll for allowing me to use the seminary's fine publications in my research and writing; to the editorial team who produced the April 2016 issue of the *Africanus* journal relating to the history of the seminary; to Scott Poblenz, Beth Isaac and Jeren Lanoue for their help in providing enrollment statistics; to Ann Elizabeth Lints for providing access to the many institutional records that are stored beneath her office; to Dennis Hollinger and Rick Lints for providing encouragement and a comfortable place to work; to Chris Anderson, Director of Marketing and Communications, for reading the manuscript and helping me to understand the seminary's marketing strategy; to my outstanding research assistants for helping me to track down information and documents; to my faculty colleagues and circle of "historian friends," many of whom have served as "conversation partners" during one phase or another of the project; and to the enormously generous friends—including David Wells, Doug Stuart, Bob Mayer, Gwenfair Adams, Ed Keazirian, Ken Swetland, Dave Horn, Tyler Lenocker, John Huffman, Bob Cooley, and Bill Wood, who did me the great honor of reading all or parts of the manuscript and who offered such helpful suggestions, corrections, and encouragement. My deepest appreciation, as always, is reserved for my amazing wife of fifty-three years. Without Janie's loving encouragement, support, and editorial suggestions, this project would never have been completed.

Two years before I was invited by Harold John Ockenga to join the Gordon-Conwell Theological Seminary faculty and to serve as its Academic Dean, our family (including my wife's father) was on sabbatical together in Oxford, England. Back in America, the year being 1976, the grand celebration of the nation's 200th birthday was already in full swing. Parades, bands, speeches and fireworks were marking the occasion. Far away from all the hoopla at home, however, our family found itself driving one beautiful Saturday morning along one of the back roads in rural England. Happening upon a small village, we noticed a tiny sign—no larger than an envelope—on which were written the words: "1000 Years."

As we entered the town we found no banners, no flags, no parades—not so much as a commemorative mug!

The contrast in English and American styles brought smiles to our faces, to be sure, but it also provided a touch of humility to our hearts. So, on the eve of our own fiftieth anniversary celebration as a seminary, perhaps we could once again benefit from a small dose of humility. Given the fast pace of American life, fifty years might seem to many like an eternity. From a more God-centered perspective, however, it is but a moment in time. Our celebrations, after all, must always and only be about God's faithfulness, goodness and love. Indeed, this modest history, with all its flaws, has no real value if it fails to point readers to the glory, majesty and amazing faithfulness of God and if it fails to serve as a reminder, to borrow the words from Charles Wesley's old hymn, that we all have "a charge to keep."

Subject Index

Names Index

Note: Italics indicate a photograph. Footnotes are indicated with an "n."

Names Index

CPSIA information can be obtained
at www.ICGtesting.com
Printed in the USA
BVHW040453210320
575608BV00005B/13